Southern Living®
ALL-TIME FAVORITE
SOUP & STEW
RECIPES

Southern Living.

ALL-TIME FAVORITE

SOUP & STEW RECIPES

Compiled and Edited by
Jean Wickstrom Liles

Oxmoor House.

Copyright 1996 by Oxmoor House, Inc.
Book Division of Southern Progress Corporation
P.O. Box 2463, Birmingham, Alabama 35201

Library of Congress Catalog Number: 96-67713
ISBN: 0-8487-2225-6
Manufactured in the United States of America
Second Printing 2000

Editor-in-Chief: Nancy Fitzpatrick Wyatt
Editorial Director, Special Interest Publications: Ann H. Harvey
Senior Foods Editor: Susan Carlisle Payne
Senior Editor, Editorial Services: Olivia Kindig Wells
Art Director: James Boone

Southern Living® ALL-TIME FAVORITE SOUP & STEW RECIPES

Menu and Recipe Consultant: Jean Wickstrom Liles
Assistant Editor: Kelly Hooper Troiano
Copy Editor: Jane Phares
Editorial Assistant: Valorie J. Cooper
Indexer: Mary Ann Laurens
Concept Designer: Melissa Jones Clark
Designer: Rita Yerby
Senior Photographers: Jim Bathie; Charles Walton IV, *Southern Living* magazine
Photographers: Ralph Anderson; Tina Evans, J. Savage Gibson, Sylvia Martin, *Southern Living* magazine
Senior Photo Stylists: Kay E. Clarke; Leslie Byars Simpson, *Southern Living* magazine
Photo Stylist: Virginia R. Cravens
Production and Distribution Director: Phillip Lee
Associate Production Managers: Theresa L. Beste, Vanessa D. Cobbs
Production Coordinator: Marianne Jordan Wilson
Production Assistant: Valerie L. Heard

Our appreciation to the editorial staff of *Southern Living* magazine and to the Southern Progress Corporation
library staff for their contributions to this volume.

Cover: Baked Potato Soup (recipe on page 43)
Page 1: Taco Soup (recipe on page 84)
Page 2: Microwave Gumbo (recipe on page 131)

Contents

Versatile
Soups and Stews

Soups and stews can be whatever you want them to be. Simple or dramatic, warm or chilled, light or robust, soups are enjoyed at all times of the day. Try a hearty stew for a Sunday night supper or a creamy soup as an elegant appetizer. These chilies and gumbos will warm you in winter, while a chilled fruit or vegetable soup will cool you in the heat of summer.

Soup's On

Soup making does not require much special equipment. A large Dutch oven or stockpot is all you'll need to prepare most of these soups and stews.

Cream soups and purees also require an electric blender or food processor to obtain the right consistency. Soups that simmer with a large number of whole herbs and spices often call for cheesecloth in which to confine spices. Called a bouquet garni, the filled spice bag allows for easy removal of the spices after the soup is cooked.

Bouquet Garni Technique

For a different method, prepare a bouquet garni for stock by wrapping aromatic herbs in leek pieces and tying with string.

Ladle Up the Soup

Our soup yields are given in cup or quart measurements rather than numbers of servings so you can be the judge, depending on how you plan to serve the soup. Allow ¾ to 1 cup soup when offering it as an appetizer. For an entrée, 1¼ to 1¾ cups is usually standard.

Serve a heavy or meaty soup as the main course. Choose a lighter, more delicate soup for an appetizer; it should have just enough taste and body to whet the appetite, especially if the main course will be filling.

Use only the freshest ingredients for savory stocks.

Homemade Made Easy

Soups and stews need not simmer for hours to be good. Several of our soup recipes call for commercially canned soup as the base, with fresh or frozen vegetables, meats, or seasonings added to enhance the flavor. These convenience foods cut preparation time but still give the finished product a "homemade" flavor.

Since some brands of soups are condensed, while other similar soups are regular strength, be sure to use the exact name and ounce-size of the soups our recipes specify. If a recipe indicates a condensed soup, the recipe will note if the soup needs diluting.

When our recipes call for chicken or beef broth, you can use our broth or stock recipes or you can substitute commercially canned broth. Just remember that canned varieties are saltier than our homemade versions, so hold extra seasonings until the end of cooking.

Bouillon cubes, granules, and powdered mixes diluted according to package directions may be used as a soup base, but these, too, are saltier than our homemade broths.

Freezing Soups and Stews

Many soups taste even better when refrigerated a day or so to allow the flavors to blend. Because of this, they are excellent make-ahead dishes for entertaining or for accommodating a busy schedule.

Most soups also freeze well, especially thick gumbos, chilies, and stews, which tend to have a large yield anyway.

• Make a double batch of soup or stew; freeze half. To freeze, cool by dividing into small portions; refrigerate until chilled.

• Use freezer containers with tight-fitting lids or freezer bags. Fill containers to ½ inch from the top to allow room for expansion.

• Select containers with wide openings so soup can be easily removed when partially thawed.

• Freeze single servings in bowls or mugs lined with heavy-duty plastic wrap; after the food is frozen, remove from bowl. Wrap with additional plastic wrap, and place in 1 large freezer bag. Label and store in freezer.

• To keep from having all of your large plastic containers in the freezer, slip a freezer bag into any container; fill with soup, and freeze. Remove the bag of frozen soup, label, and store in freezer.

• Use the frozen soup within 3 or 4 months for optimum flavor.

• Thaw frozen soups in the refrigerator or microwave oven.

Homemade Stocks

Soups and stews are only as good as the stock from which they're made.

Stocks are usually made by slowly simmering meaty bones and vegetables until they have yielded most of their flavor to the water in which they've been cooked.

The liquid is then strained off, and the stock is either served as a hearty broth or used as a delicate background for other flavorings in soups and sauces.

Here are methods for making four basic stocks: beef, chicken, fish, and vegetable. Although they take a long time to make, once preparation has begun, they require little supervision. And each batch yields ample quantities that can be refrigerated or frozen in small containers for future use. Each type of homemade stock lends itself to a host of uses.

10 Tips for High-Yield Stocks

When making stock, the goal is to produce a foundation that's clear and distinctly flavored. Follow these cardinal rules when making stock.

• Use a heavyweight stockpot that holds 10 to 20 quarts of liquid.

• To produce a more flavorful stock, cut all vegetables in pieces; remove excess fat from bones; and crack large bones.

Cut vegetables to allow flavor and nutrients to leach into the stock.

• If making fish stock, use the heads, bones, and trimmings from any mild whitefish; avoid oily, strong-flavored fish, such as salmon and mackerel, as they will yield a milky, bitter-tasting stock.

• When making beef stock, roast bones and vegetables in the oven only until golden brown; overbrowning will damage the stock's flavor and darken its color.

Brown bones for a dark-colored stock.

• To coax maximum flavor from meat, bones, and vegetables, cook these ingredients in a cold liquid. If the ingredients have been browned first, allow them to cool slightly before adding them to the cold cooking liquid.

• It's best to bring stock to a boil slowly; then reduce heat, and simmer gently throughout cooking time. Rapid boiling will produce a murky, unpalatable stock. Gentle simmering, on the other hand, extracts flavors from ingredients and produces a relatively clear, well-flavored stock.

• To achieve a clear stock, it is important to carefully skim the fat and foam from the surface of the mixture as it rises to the top during cooking. To make the skimming easier, vegetables and "aromatics" (seasonings) are best added after about one-fourth of the cooking time has elapsed. Once the vegetables are added, do not skim the fat again unless it is necessary.

After chilling, skim solidified fat from stock.

• As a stock simmers, its flavor becomes more pronounced; therefore, you should add salt only after stock is finished cooking.

• Homemade stock may be refrigerated up to four days. For longer storage, cool and freeze up to four months, with the exception of fish and vegetable stocks, which can be frozen only up to two months.

• Degrease stock before freezing; frozen fat can turn rancid. A fat-off ladle allows you to skim fat from stocks. Ladle the defatted mixture into containers, such as plastic bags or ice-cube trays, for convenient quantities. Each cube yields approximately 2 tablespoons of stock.

Freeze stock in ice-cube trays for convenience.

Beef Stock

5 pounds beef or veal bones
2 large carrots, quartered
2 large onions, quartered
4 stalks celery, quartered
4 quarts water, divided
3 tablespoons tomato paste
6 to 8 sprigs fresh parsley
3 to 4 sprigs fresh thyme
4 whole cloves
½ teaspoon black peppercorns
1 bay leaf
2 cloves garlic, crushed

Place first 4 ingredients in a large roasting pan; bake at 500° for 1 hour, turning mixture occasionally with a large spatula.

Transfer mixture to a large stockpot; set aside. Discard drippings from roasting pan.

Add 1 quart water to roasting pan; bring to a boil over medium-high heat, stirring to loosen pieces. Pour into stockpot; add 3 quarts water and remaining ingredients. Bring to a boil; cover, reduce heat, and simmer 2 hours.

Line a large wire-mesh strainer with a double layer of cheesecloth; place in a large bowl. Pour stock through strainer; discard solids. Cool stock.

Cover and chill stock; remove and discard solidified fat from top of stock. Store stock in refrigerator up to 2 days, or freeze up to 4 months. **Yield: 2 quarts.**

Quick Full-Bodied Stock

2 (14½-ounce) cans ready-to-serve chicken or beef broth
1 large carrot, scraped and sliced
1 medium onion, sliced
1 bay leaf
3 or 4 sprigs fresh parsley

Remove solidified fat from top of broth, if necessary, and discard. Combine broth and remaining ingredients in a medium saucepan.

Bring mixture to a boil over medium heat; cover, reduce heat, and simmer 25 minutes.

Pour through a wire-mesh strainer into a bowl; discard solids. Cool stock. Cover; chill up to 2 days, or freeze up to 4 months. **Yield: 2 cups.**

Vegetable Stock

4½ quarts water
3 medium onions, chopped
5 stalks celery, sliced
1 pound carrots, scraped and sliced
1 small bunch parsley
1 medium turnip, chopped
3 cloves garlic, quartered
3 bay leaves
1 teaspoon dried thyme

Combine all ingredients in a stockpot. Bring to a boil; cover, reduce heat, and simmer 1½ to 2 hours. Uncover and continue cooking 2 hours.

Pour mixture through a large wire-mesh strainer into a large bowl, discarding vegetables. Cool stock slightly. Cover and chill up to 2 days, or freeze up to 2 months. **Yield: 1 quart.**

Chicken Stock

4 pounds chicken pieces
1 pound chicken wings
4 quarts water
2 onions, peeled and quartered
4 stalks celery with tops, cut into 2-inch pieces
4 carrots, scraped and cut into 2-inch pieces
1 large bay leaf
6 sprigs fresh parsley
1 tablespoon fresh thyme or 1 teaspoon dried thyme
6 sprigs fresh dill or ½ teaspoon dried dillweed
½ teaspoon black peppercorns

Combine chicken and water in a large stockpot; bring to a boil, skimming surface to remove excess fat and foam.

Add onion and remaining ingredients. Return to a boil; reduce heat, and simmer, uncovered, 2 hours, skimming surface to remove fat.

Line a large wire-mesh strainer with a double layer of cheesecloth; place in a large bowl. Pour stock through strainer; reserve chicken for other uses, and discard remaining solids. Cool stock.

Cover and chill stock. Remove and discard solidified fat from top of stock. Cover; chill up to 2 days, or freeze up to 4 months. **Yield: 2 quarts.**

Chicken Stock Technique

Strain stock through a colander lined with several layers of moistened cheesecloth.

Fish Stock

2 leeks
6 to 9 sprigs fresh parsley
1 large bay leaf
4 sprigs fresh basil
4 sprigs fresh rosemary
3 sprigs fresh thyme
2 (2- x ½-inch) strips lemon rind
2 (2- x ½-inch) strips orange rind
2 tablespoons margarine
1 medium onion, sliced
½ carrot, sliced
2 stalks celery with leaves, coarsely chopped
3 pounds fish bones and shrimp shells
6 whole peppercorns
2 quarts water
1 cup dry white wine
½ teaspoon salt

Remove roots, outer leaves, and green tops of leeks, reserving 2 pieces of tops. Split white portion in half lengthwise, and wash; set aside. Trim reserved green pieces; place parsley and next 6 ingredients on top of 1 green piece; top with other green piece, and tie with string. (See bouquet garni technique on page 6.) Set bouquet garni aside.

Melt margarine in a stockpot over medium heat. Add leek, onion, carrot, and celery; cook, stirring constantly, until tender. Add bouquet garni, fish bones and shrimp shells, and next 3 ingredients to stockpot. Bring mixture to a boil; cover, reduce heat, and simmer 35 to 45 minutes.

Line a wire-mesh strainer with a double layer of cheesecloth; place in a large bowl. Pour stock through strainer, discarding solids. Stir in salt; cool stock slightly.

Cover and chill stock. Remove and discard solidified fat from top of stock. Cover stock, and chill in the refrigerator up to 2 days, or freeze up to 2 months. **Yield: 1½ quarts.**

Light Soups

When your winter meal needs a warm broth-based soup or your summer menu calls for a refreshing tomato-based gazpacho, choose one of these lighter soups.

Egg Drop Soup, Fancy French Onion Soup, Easy Tortilla Soup

Shrimp-Cream Cheese Gazpacho, Summer Garden Soup, Calico Cheese Soup

Southwestern Scallop Broth with Black Beans and Cilantro, Beer-Cheese Soup

Spicy Thai Lobster Soup, Tomato Soup with Herbed Croutons

Tortilla Soup (page 16)

Egg Drop Soup

4 cups hot water
1 (10½-ounce) can condensed chicken broth, undiluted
1 (4-ounce) can sliced mushrooms, drained
2 cloves garlic
1 teaspoon soy sauce
1 teaspoon chicken-flavored bouillon granules
⅛ teaspoon ground white pepper
2 large eggs, beaten
⅓ cup sliced green onions

Combine first 6 ingredients in a deep 3-quart baking dish. Cover with heavy-duty plastic wrap; fold back a small edge of wrap to allow steam to escape. Microwave at HIGH 10 to 12 minutes or until boiling.

Add pepper, stirring well. Gradually pour beaten eggs in a thin stream into soup, stirring constantly. (The eggs form lacy strands as they cook.)

Cover and let stand 3 minutes. Remove garlic; sprinkle with green onions. **Yield: 1½ quarts.**

Egg Drop Soup for Two

1⅓ cups water
1 (10½-ounce) can condensed chicken broth, undiluted
1 teaspoon soy sauce
1 tablespoon cornstarch
2 tablespoons water
1 large egg, beaten
1 tablespoon dry sherry
Thinly sliced green onions

Combine first 3 ingredients in a medium saucepan; bring to a boil.

Combine cornstarch and 2 tablespoons water, stirring well; add to broth mixture. Boil 1 minute over medium heat, stirring occasionally.

Combine egg and sherry; slowly pour egg mixture into boiling soup, stirring constantly. (The egg forms lacy strands as it cooks.) Ladle soup into bowls, and sprinkle with green onions. Serve immediately. **Yield: 2⅔ cups.**

Fancy French Onion Soup

2 large Vidalia or other sweet onions, thinly sliced
1 clove garlic, crushed
¼ cup butter or margarine, melted
1 tablespoon all-purpose flour
2 (10½-ounce) cans condensed beef broth, undiluted
2 cups water
¼ teaspoon pepper
¼ cup Madeira
6 (¾-inch-thick) slices French bread, toasted
1 cup (4 ounces) shredded smoked mozzarella cheese
1 cup (4 ounces) shredded mozzarella cheese
Grated Parmesan cheese

Cook onion and garlic in butter in a Dutch oven over medium heat 10 to 15 minutes or until very tender.

Add flour, stirring until smooth. Gradually add beef broth and water. Bring to a boil; cover, reduce heat, and simmer 15 minutes. Stir in pepper and wine. Remove from heat.

Place 6 ovenproof serving bowls on a baking sheet. Place 1 toasted bread slice in each bowl; ladle soup into bowls.

Sprinkle each serving evenly with mozzarella cheeses; sprinkle with Parmesan cheese. Broil 5½ inches from heat (with electric oven door partially opened) 1 minute or until cheese melts. **Yield: 1½ quarts.**

Fancy French Onion Soup

French Onion Soup

1 tablespoon butter or margarine, softened
   and divided
6 (¾-inch-thick) slices French bread
¾ teaspoon garlic powder, divided
1 tablespoon grated Parmesan cheese, divided
1½ pounds onions, sliced (about 5 cups)
¼ cup butter or margarine, melted
2 (10½-ounce) cans condensed beef broth,
   undiluted
1⅓ cups water
2 teaspoons Worcestershire sauce
⅛ teaspoon cracked pepper
⅛ teaspoon curry powder
Pinch of garlic powder
½ cup (2 ounces) shredded mozzarella cheese

Spread ½ teaspoon softened butter on one
side of each slice of bread; sprinkle with ⅛ teaspoon garlic powder.

Place bread on a baking sheet; bake at 300°
for 15 to 20 minutes. Sprinkle with ½ teaspoon
Parmesan cheese. Set aside.

Separate onion into rings; cook in ¼ cup butter in a Dutch oven over medium heat 25 to 30
minutes, stirring frequently. Add beef broth and
next 5 ingredients; bring to a boil. Cover, reduce
heat, and simmer 30 minutes.

Fill 6 soup bowls with soup. Sprinkle each
serving evenly with mozzarella cheese, and top
with a bread slice. **Yield: about 1½ quarts.**

Easy Tortilla Soup

½ cup chopped onion
1 clove garlic, minced
1 tablespoon vegetable oil
3 medium zucchini, sliced
1 quart ready-to-serve chicken broth
1 (16-ounce) can stewed tomatoes, undrained
1 (15-ounce) can tomato sauce
1 (12-ounce) can whole kernel corn,
   undrained
1 teaspoon ground cumin
½ teaspoon pepper
Tortilla chips
½ cup (2 ounces) shredded Monterey Jack or
   Cheddar cheese

Cook onion and garlic in oil in a Dutch oven.
Add zucchini and next 6 ingredients; bring to a
boil. Cover, reduce heat, and simmer 15 to 20
minutes.

Spoon soup into bowls; add tortilla chips and
cheese. **Yield: 2¼ quarts.**

Stock Options

• If you don't have time to make
homemade stock, give canned broth
a flavor boost by simmering it with
aromatic vegetables for 30 minutes.
• To defat commercial beef or chick-
en broth, place the unopened can in
the refrigerator at least 1 hour
before using. Open the can, and
skim off the layer of solidified fat.

Easy Tortilla Soup

Tortilla Soup

(pictured on page 11)

1 dried ancho chile
¼ cup olive oil
4 corn tortillas, cut into 1-inch pieces
1 large onion, coarsely chopped
1 medium-size green pepper, seeded and
    chopped
3 cloves garlic, minced
1 quart ready-to-serve chicken broth
½ teaspoon ground cumin
½ teaspoon freshly ground black pepper
2 tomatoes, unpeeled and chopped
2 tablespoons chopped fresh cilantro
1 tablespoon chopped fresh parsley

Remove stem and seeds from chile; cook chile in hot oil in a Dutch oven until soft. Remove chile, and chop, reserving drippings in Dutch oven.

Fry tortilla pieces in drippings until brown. Remove tortillas, and drain, reserving drippings in Dutch oven.

Cook onion, green pepper, and garlic in drippings until tender. Add chicken broth, cumin, and pepper. Bring to a boil; cover, reduce heat, and simmer 20 minutes.

Stir in reserved chile and tomato; simmer 10 minutes. Before serving, stir in cilantro and parsley.

Place fried tortilla pieces in individual soup bowls, reserving one-fourth of chips; add soup. Top with reserved chips. **Yield: 1½ quarts.**

Southwestern Scallop Broth with Black Beans and Cilantro

¼ cup dried black beans
10 cups fish stock, divided
¼ cup olive oil
2 cloves garlic, minced
1 medium jicama, chopped
1 stalk celery, chopped
1 medium onion, chopped
1 carrot, scraped and chopped
1 bay leaf
1½ pounds bay scallops
8 tomatillos, ground
2 teaspoons chopped fresh cilantro
1 tablespoon tequila
½ teaspoon salt
¼ teaspoon pepper
Corn tortillas (optional)

Sort and wash beans. Cover beans with water; soak overnight. Drain beans.

Bring 5 cups fish stock to a boil. Add beans; cover and simmer 2 to 3 hours or until desired degree of doneness. Remove from heat. Cool beans in fish stock; set aside.

Heat olive oil in a large Dutch oven over medium-high heat. Add garlic and next 6 ingredients, and cook until vegetables are transparent. Add tomatillo, cilantro, and remaining 5 cups fish stock; bring to a boil.

Strain and rinse black beans; discard stock. Drain and add to vegetable-broth mixture. Bring to a boil; add tequila, salt, and pepper. Remove bay leaf. **Yield: 3 quarts.**

Note: Broth can be garnished with corn tortillas cut into ⅛-inch strips and deep-fried until crisp, if desired.

Bacon, Lettuce, and Tomato Soup

Bacon, Lettuce, and Tomato Soup

3 beef-flavored bouillon cubes
3 cups hot water
8 slices bacon, cut into 1-inch pieces
⅓ cup chopped onion
⅓ cup chopped celery
5 ripe tomatoes, peeled and coarsely chopped
1 tablespoon Worcestershire sauce
½ teaspoon garlic salt
½ teaspoon dried parsley flakes
¼ teaspoon dried thyme
¼ teaspoon pepper
Dash of hot sauce
2 cups shredded lettuce
Seasoned croutons

Dissolve bouillon cubes in hot water; set aside.

Cook bacon in a Dutch oven until crisp; remove bacon, reserving 2 tablespoons drippings in Dutch oven. Drain bacon on paper towels.

Add onion and celery to drippings, and cook, stirring frequently, until transparent; drain. Add bouillon, tomato, and next 6 ingredients; bring to a boil. Reduce heat, and simmer, uncovered, 20 to 25 minutes. Add lettuce, and cook 2 minutes or until lettuce wilts.

Top each serving with bacon and croutons. Serve immediately. **Yield: 1¼ quarts.**

Turtle Soup

¼ cup butter or margarine, melted
1 pound ground turtle meat
⅓ pound ground veal
1¼ cups diced onion
1 cup diced celery
3 cloves garlic, minced
1½ teaspoons ground cumin
1 teaspoon dried oregano
½ teaspoon dried thyme
½ teaspoon salt
½ teaspoon pepper
3 bay leaves
1 (16-ounce) can tomato puree
1 quart ready-to-serve beef broth
1 cup butter or margarine
¾ cup all-purpose flour
Condiments: dry sherry, chopped hard-
    cooked eggs

Combine first 3 ingredients in a Dutch oven; cook over medium heat until meat is browned, stirring until it crumbles.

Add onion and next 8 ingredients; cook, stirring often, until vegetables are tender. Stir in tomato puree; cook 10 minutes.

Add beef broth, and bring to a boil; reduce heat, and simmer, uncovered, 1 hour. Remove bay leaves. Remove soup from heat, and set aside.

Melt 1 cup butter in a Dutch oven over medium heat. Add flour; cook, stirring constantly, until mixture is chocolate-colored (about 25 minutes). Add turtle mixture; cook until thickened, stirring often. Serve soup with condiments, if desired. **Yield: about 2 quarts.**

Spicy Thai Lobster Soup

2 fresh lobster tails
1 tablespoon ground ginger
½ teaspoon ground red pepper
1 tablespoon peanut oil
5 cups ready-to-serve chicken broth
1 tablespoon coarsely grated lime rind
⅓ cup long-grain rice, uncooked
1 cup unsweetened coconut milk
6 large fresh mushrooms, sliced
½ cup chopped onion
1 tablespoon chopped fresh cilantro
2 tablespoons lime juice
Garnishes: chopped green onions, fresh
    cilantro sprigs

Remove lobster from shell; slice. Set aside.

Cook ground ginger and red pepper in peanut oil in a large saucepan over medium heat 1 minute. Add chicken broth and lime rind.

Bring to a boil. Stir in rice; cover, reduce heat, and simmer 15 to 20 minutes.

Add coconut milk and next 3 ingredients; cook 5 minutes, stirring occasionally.

Add lobster; cook 3 to 5 minutes. Remove from heat, and stir in lime juice. Spoon into bowls; garnish, if desired. **Yield: 1½ quarts.**

Note: You may substitute 1 pound unpeeled, medium-size fresh shrimp for lobster tails. Peel shrimp, and devein, if desired.

Keep Cilantro Fresh

Extend the life of fresh cilantro, also known as coriander leaves, by placing it, stem down, in a glass jar with a small amount of water. Cover the leaves with a plastic bag, and refrigerate up to one week, changing the water every 2 days.

Summer Garden Soup

Summer Garden Soup

2¼ cups tomato juice
1 medium carrot, scraped and sliced
1 stalk celery, sliced
½ cup seeded, chopped cucumber
2 green onions, chopped
1 (¼-inch-thick) slice lemon
½ teaspoon celery salt
½ teaspoon Worcestershire sauce
⅛ teaspoon hot pepper sauce
Garnish: green onion fans

Combine first 9 ingredients in container of a food processor or electric blender; process until smooth.

Cover and chill. Ladle soup into individual serving bowls, or store in refrigerator in a tightly covered container up to 3 days. Garnish, if desired. **Yield: 3 cups.**

Tomato Soup with Herbed Croutons

Tomato Soup with Herbed Croutons

½ cup chopped onion
3 tablespoons butter or margarine, melted
3 tablespoons all-purpose flour
1 cup ready-to-serve chicken broth
1 (28-ounce) can Italian-style tomatoes, undrained
3 tablespoons tomato paste
1 tablespoon minced fresh parsley
1 tablespoon sugar
1 teaspoon salt
½ teaspoon dried basil
¼ teaspoon pepper
1 bay leaf
Herbed Croutons
Garnish: fresh basil sprigs

Cook onion in butter in a Dutch oven 3 minutes or until tender. Reduce heat to low; add flour, stirring until smooth. Cook 1 minute, stirring constantly.

Add chicken broth gradually; cook over medium heat, stirring constantly, until thickened and bubbly.

Add tomatoes and next 7 ingredients; stir well. Bring to a boil; cover, reduce heat, and simmer 30 minutes. Remove bay leaf.

Spoon one-third of tomato mixture into container of an electric blender; cover and process until smooth. Repeat procedure twice with remaining tomato mixture.

Ladle soup into individual serving bowls. Top with Herbed Croutons, and garnish, if desired. **Yield: 3½ cups.**

Herbed Croutons

2 slices white bread
1 tablespoon butter or margarine, melted
1 tablespoon grated Parmesan cheese
½ teaspoon dried basil

Trim crust from bread slices; reserve for another use. Brush butter over bread slices; sprinkle evenly with cheese and basil. Cut each slice into 4 squares; cut each square into 2 triangles.

Place on an ungreased baking sheet; bake at 350° for 10 to 12 minutes or until croutons are dry and lightly browned. **Yield: 16 croutons.**

Shrimp-Cream Cheese Gazpacho

5 cups water
1½ pounds unpeeled small fresh shrimp
2 quarts tomato juice
1 bunch green onions, chopped
2 cucumbers, peeled, seeded, and chopped
4 tomatoes, peeled, seeded, and chopped
1 avocado, peeled and chopped
1 (8-ounce) package cream cheese, cubed
¼ cup lemon juice or white wine vinegar
2 tablespoons sugar
½ teaspoon hot sauce
Garnishes: cucumber slices, sour cream, shrimp

Bring water to a boil; add shrimp, and cook 3 to 5 minutes or until shrimp turn pink. Drain well; rinse with cold water. Chill.

Peel shrimp, and devein, if desired. (Set aside about 10 shrimp for garnishing, if desired.)

Combine shrimp, tomato juice, and next 8 ingredients in a large bowl; cover gazpacho, and chill at least 3 hours. Garnish, if desired. **Yield: 3¼ quarts.**

Gazpacho

1 (10¾-ounce) can tomato soup, undiluted
1½ cups tomato juice
1¼ cups water
½ to 1 cup chopped cucumber
½ to 1 cup chopped tomato
½ cup chopped green pepper
½ cup chopped onion
2 tablespoons white wine vinegar
1 tablespoon commercial Italian dressing
1 tablespoon lemon or lime juice
1 clove garlic, minced
¼ teaspoon pepper
¼ teaspoon hot sauce

Combine all ingredients; cover and chill at least 6 hours. **Yield: 1½ quarts.**

Spicy Gazpacho

4 (6-ounce) cans spicy hot tomato juice
1½ cups tomato juice
1 cup chopped tomato
¾ cup chopped cucumber
½ cup minced green pepper
2 tablespoons minced green onions
3 tablespoons white wine vinegar
1 tablespoon lemon juice
¼ teaspoon lemon-pepper seasoning
¼ teaspoon coarsely ground black pepper
Dash of hot sauce
Seasoned Croutons
Additional chopped tomato, green onions, and
    cucumber

Combine first 11 ingredients in a large bowl; stir well. Cover and chill at least 2 hours.

Pour gazpacho into chilled individual soup bowls. Top each serving with Seasoned Croutons and additional chopped tomato, green onions, and cucumber. **Yield: 1½ quarts.**

Seasoned Croutons

¼ cup butter or margarine
2 teaspoons dried Italian seasoning
½ teaspoon garlic salt
4 (¾-inch) slices French bread, cubed

Melt butter in a large skillet; stir in Italian seasoning and garlic salt. Add bread cubes, tossing to coat well. Remove from heat.

Spread bread cubes evenly on an ungreased 15- x 10- x 1-inch jellyroll pan. Bake at 300° for 30 minutes or until crisp; remove from pan, and cool. **Yield: about 2 cups.**

Seasoned Croutons Techniques

Cut French bread slices into ¾-inch cubes.

Stir croutons occasionally during baking.

Spicy Gazpacho

Beer-Cheese Soup

6 cups milk
2 (12-ounce) cans beer, divided
5 (8-ounce) jars process cheese spread
1 (10½-ounce) can condensed chicken broth, undiluted
1 teaspoon Worcestershire sauce
3 dashes of hot sauce
⅓ cup cornstarch

Combine milk and 2½ cups beer in a large Dutch oven. Cook over low heat, stirring constantly, until thoroughly heated. Add cheese spread and next 3 ingredients. Cook over low heat, stirring constantly, until heated.

Combine cornstarch and remaining beer. Add to cheese mixture; simmer, stirring constantly, until thickened (do not boil). **Yield: 4 quarts.**

Cheese Velvet Soup

6 ounces Brie cheese
½ cup finely chopped celery
½ cup finely chopped carrot
¼ cup finely chopped onion
½ cup butter or margarine, melted
½ cup all-purpose flour
2 cups ready-to-serve chicken broth
1 teaspoon dried thyme
1 bay leaf
½ cup whipping cream
Garnish: shredded carrot

Cut rind from Brie; set cheese aside.
Cook celery, carrot, and onion in butter in a saucepan over medium heat, stirring constantly, until tender.
Add flour, and cook over low heat 1 minute, stirring constantly. Gradually stir in chicken broth, dried thyme, and bay leaf. Cook, stirring constantly, until mixture is thickened and bubbly.

Add cheese, stirring until smooth. Add whipping cream, and heat thoroughly. Remove bay leaf. Garnish, if desired. **Yield: 3 cups.**

Calico Cheese Soup

½ cup finely chopped carrot
½ cup finely chopped green pepper
½ cup finely chopped sweet red pepper
½ cup finely chopped celery
2 tablespoons minced onion
¼ cup butter or margarine, melted
3 tablespoons all-purpose flour
2 cups milk
2 cups ready-to-serve chicken broth
2 cups (8 ounces) shredded sharp Cheddar cheese
Salt and pepper to taste
Commercial seasoned croutons
½ cup (2 ounces) finely shredded sharp Cheddar cheese

Combine first 4 ingredients in a medium saucepan; add water to cover. Bring to a boil; cover, reduce heat, and simmer 3 to 5 minutes or until vegetables are tender. Drain and set aside.

Cook onion in butter in a large saucepan over medium heat until tender. Reduce heat to low; add flour, stirring until smooth. Cook 1 minute, stirring constantly. Combine milk and chicken broth; gradually add to flour mixture. Cook over medium heat, stirring constantly, until mixture is slightly thickened. Stir in 2 cups shredded cheese; cook, stirring constantly, until cheese melts. Add reserved vegetables and salt and pepper to taste. Cook until thoroughly heated.

Ladle soup into individual serving bowls. Top with croutons and cheese. **Yield: 1½ quarts.**

Calico Cheese Soup

Vegetable-Cheese Soup

Vegetable-Cheese Soup

2 stalks celery, chopped
2 carrots, scraped and diced
1 medium onion, chopped
1 cup chopped cauliflower
½ cup chopped broccoli
1 clove garlic, minced
½ cup butter or margarine, melted
½ cup all-purpose flour
3 cups ready-to-serve chicken broth
1 tablespoon Worcestershire sauce
½ teaspoon pepper
2½ cups milk
2 cups (8 ounces) shredded sharp Cheddar
    cheese
¼ cup sliced almonds, toasted

Cook first 6 ingredients in butter in a Dutch oven until crisp-tender; add flour, stirring until smooth. Cook 1 minute, stirring constantly.

Add chicken broth gradually; cook over medium heat, stirring constantly, until mixture is thickened and bubbly. Cover, reduce heat, and simmer 20 minutes or until vegetables are tender.

Add Worcestershire sauce and next 3 ingredients. Cook over low heat 10 minutes, stirring occasionally. Top each serving with sliced almonds, and serve immediately. **Yield: 2 quarts.**

Creams & Purees

Let your blender, processor, and soup pot refine vegetables and fruits into their purest, smoothest forms. Serve these soups as elegant appetizers, light lunches, or sweet endings to dinner.

Artichoke Cream Soup, Creamy Asparagus Soup, Cold Dill Soup

Yellow Squash Soup, Cream Pea Soup, Cantaloupe Soup, Strawberry-Banana Soup

Cream of Broccoli Soup, Chilled Carrot-Mint Soup, Velvety Roquefort Vichyssoise

Baked Potato Soup, Sweet Potato Soup, Watercress-Zucchini Soup

Cream of Roasted Sweet Red Pepper Soup (page 39)

Artichoke Cream Soup

Artichoke Cream Soup

6 artichokes
1 lemon, sliced
1 teaspoon salt
1 quart ready-to-serve chicken broth
½ cup butter or margarine
1 onion, finely chopped
½ cup chopped celery
1 tablespoon minced garlic
2 cups dry white wine
1 quart whipping cream
⅛ teaspoon seasoned salt
¼ teaspoon freshly ground pepper
Pumpernickel Croutons
Garnish: peeled tomato strips

Wash artichokes by plunging them up and down in cold water. Cut off stem end, and trim about ½ inch from top of each artichoke. Remove and discard any loose bottom leaves.

Place artichokes in a large stainless steel Dutch oven; cover with water, and add lemon and 1 teaspoon salt. Bring to a boil; cover, reduce heat, and simmer 35 minutes. Drain well.

Spread leaves apart; remove fuzzy thistle (choke) with a spoon, and discard. Remove all leaves, leaving artichoke bottoms intact; set leaves aside. Finely chop artichoke bottoms, and set aside.

Combine artichoke leaves and chicken broth. Bring to a boil; cover, reduce heat, and simmer 40 minutes.

Pour broth mixture through a large wire-mesh strainer into a container, discarding solids; set artichoke stock aside.

Melt butter in a Dutch oven over medium-high heat; add onion, celery, and garlic, and cook, stirring constantly, 10 minutes or until tender.

Add chopped artichoke bottoms and wine; cook over medium heat about 2 minutes. Add artichoke stock, and cook over low heat 20 minutes, stirring occasionally.

Pour half of broth mixture into container of an electric blender; cover and process until smooth, stopping once to scrape down sides. Pour mixture into a large bowl. Repeat procedure with remaining mixture; return all mixture to Dutch oven.

Add whipping cream, seasoned salt, and pepper; cook over low heat until thoroughly heated. Top each serving with Pumpernickel Croutons. Garnish, if desired. **Yield: 2¼ quarts.**

Pumpernickel Croutons
4 slices dark pumpernickel bread

Cut bread into desired shapes; place on a baking sheet.

Bake at 325° for 20 minutes or until crisp. **Yield: 1 cup.**

Serve with Style
Spark appetites by serving soup in surprising containers.
• Use hollowed-out fruits or vegetables such as peppers, acorn squash, pumpkins, tomatoes, or cantaloupes.
• Make edible bowls by scooping out the center of French rolls or small round bread loaves.
• Serve cold soups from chilled goblets or punch cups.

Creamy Asparagus Soup

½ cup chopped onion
1 cup sliced celery
3 cloves garlic, crushed
3 tablespoons butter or margarine, melted
2 (14.5-ounce) cans cut asparagus, undrained
1 (16-ounce) can sliced potatoes, drained
1 (14½-ounce) can ready-to-serve chicken
　　broth
1 teaspoon white vinegar
1 teaspoon salt
½ teaspoon ground black pepper
¼ teaspoon ground red pepper
½ teaspoon dried basil
1 cup milk
½ cup sour cream (optional)
Garnish: celery leaves

Cook first 3 ingredients in butter in a Dutch oven over medium-high heat, stirring constantly, until tender. Add asparagus and next 7 ingredients.

Bring to a boil, stirring often. Reduce heat, and simmer 10 minutes, stirring often. Cool slightly.

Pour half of mixture into container of an electric blender; cover and process until smooth, stopping once to scrape down sides. Transfer mixture to another container. Repeat procedure.

Return asparagus mixture to Dutch oven. Stir in milk; cook just until thoroughly heated (do not boil). If desired, dollop each serving with sour cream, and garnish. **Yield: 2 quarts.**

Note: You may substitute 2 medium potatoes, cooked, peeled, and sliced, for canned sliced potatoes.

Chilled Avocado Soup

2 ripe avocados, peeled and seeded
1 (14½-ounce) can ready-to-serve chicken
    broth
1 (8-ounce) carton plain yogurt
2 tablespoons lemon juice, divided
1 ripe avocado, peeled, seeded, and finely
    chopped
Coarsely ground pepper

  Position knife blade in food processor bowl;
add 2 avocados. Process until smooth, scraping
sides of processor bowl once.
  Combine pureed avocado, chicken broth,
yogurt, and 1 tablespoon lemon juice in a large
bowl. Cover and chill.
  Toss chopped avocado with remaining 1 tablespoon lemon juice; set aside. Just before serving
soup, stir in chopped avocado and ground pepper.
Yield: 1¼ quarts.

Borscht

1 (16-ounce) can whole beets, undrained
1 (10½-ounce) can condensed chicken broth,
    undiluted
1 (8-ounce) carton sour cream
⅛ teaspoon ground white pepper
1½ teaspoons lemon juice
2 tablespoons chopped chives

  Combine beets and chicken broth in container
of an electric blender or food processor. Cover
and process until smooth.
  Combine beet puree, sour cream, pepper, and
lemon juice; stir well. Cover and chill. Sprinkle
each serving of soup with chives. **Yield: 1 quart.**

Cream of Broccoli Soup

2 cups water
1 (16-ounce) package frozen broccoli cuts
½ cup chopped onion
½ cup butter or margarine, melted
½ cup all-purpose flour
6 cups milk
4 chicken-flavored bouillon cubes
1 teaspoon ground white pepper

  Bring water to a boil in a medium saucepan;
add broccoli. Cover, reduce heat, and simmer 5
minutes. Remove from heat, and set aside.
  Cook onion in butter in a Dutch oven over
low heat 10 minutes or until tender. Add flour; stir
until smooth. Cook 1 minute, stirring constantly.
  Add milk and bouillon cubes; cook over
medium heat, stirring constantly, until thickened.
Add broccoli, cooking water, and pepper. Simmer 20 to 30 minutes, stirring occasionally.
Yield: 2¼ quarts.

Carrot Cream Soup

(pictured on page 37)

3 cups sliced carrot
1 cup chopped onion
3 cups ready-to-serve chicken broth
¼ teaspoon ground white pepper
1 cup whipping cream
Garnishes: ground nutmeg, carrot curls, fresh
    chives

  Combine first 3 ingredients in a Dutch oven;
cover and cook over medium heat 25 minutes.
  Spoon half of carrot mixture into a food processor or electric blender; process until smooth.
Repeat procedure with remaining mixture.
  Stir in white pepper; cover and chill soup thoroughly. Stir in whipping cream; ladle into individual
soup bowls. Garnish, if desired. **Yield: 1¼ quarts.**

Chilled Carrot-Mint Soup

Chilled Carrot-Mint Soup

2 cups sliced carrot
2 tablespoons water
½ teaspoon onion powder
2 cups ready-to-serve chicken broth
1 tablespoon sugar
¼ to ½ teaspoon salt
2 tablespoons minced fresh mint
1 cup milk
Garnishes: sour cream, fresh mint sprigs,
    carrot curls

Combine sliced carrot, water, and onion powder in a 1-quart bowl. Cover with heavy-duty plastic wrap; fold back a small edge of wrap to allow steam to escape. Microwave at HIGH 6 to 8 minutes or until carrot is tender.

Spoon carrot mixture into container of an electric blender. Add chicken broth, sugar, salt, and mint; cover and process at high until mixture is smooth. Pour into a bowl; cover and chill.

Stir milk into chilled soup. Spoon into serving bowls. Garnish, if desired. **Yield: 1 quart.**

Creamy Carrot Soup

Creamy Carrot Soup

1 medium onion, chopped
2 tablespoons butter or margarine, melted
2 pounds carrots, scraped and sliced
3 cups ready-to-serve chicken broth, divided
1 cup half-and-half
¼ teaspoon coarsely ground pepper
Pinch of salt
1 (8-ounce) carton plain yogurt
1 tablespoon minced fresh dill or 1 teaspoon dried dillweed
Garnish: fresh dill sprigs

Cook onion in butter in a Dutch oven over medium-high heat, stirring constantly, until tender. Add carrot and 1 cup chicken broth; bring to a boil over medium heat. Cover, reduce heat, and simmer 8 minutes or until carrot is tender.

Spoon carrot mixture into container of an electric blender; cover and process until smooth. Return to Dutch oven; add remaining chicken broth, half-and-half, pepper, and salt. Cook over low heat, stirring constantly, until thoroughly heated. Stir in yogurt (at room temperature) and dill with a wire whisk. Serve hot or chilled. Garnish, if desired. **Yield: 2 quarts.**

Microwave Directions:

Place onion and butter in a 3-quart baking dish. Cover with heavy-duty plastic wrap; fold back a small edge of wrap to allow steam to escape. Microwave at HIGH 2 minutes. Stir in carrot; cover and microwave at HIGH 12 minutes or until tender, turning dish after 6 minutes.

Spoon carrot mixture and 1 cup chicken broth into container of an electric blender; cover and process until smooth. Return to baking dish; add remaining chicken broth, half-and-half, pepper, and salt. Microwave at HIGH 8 to 10 minutes.

Stir in yogurt (at room temperature) and dill with a wire whisk. Serve hot or chilled. Garnish, if desired.

Cauliflower Soup

1 cup chopped cauliflower
2 teaspoons minced shallots
3 cups ready-to-serve chicken broth
¼ cup butter or margarine
¼ cup all-purpose flour
½ cup half-and-half
1 tablespoon minced parsley
⅛ teaspoon dried tarragon
⅛ teaspoon pepper

Combine first 3 ingredients in a large saucepan; bring to a boil. Cover, reduce heat, and simmer 15 minutes. Remove from heat, and drain vegetables, reserving liquid. Set both aside.

Melt butter in a heavy saucepan over low heat; add flour, stirring until smooth. Cook 1 minute, stirring constantly. Gradually stir in reserved liquid; cook over medium heat, stirring constantly, until thickened and bubbly.

Stir in reserved vegetables, half-and-half, and remaining ingredients; cook until thoroughly heated. **Yield: 1 quart.**

Hot Soup Tips

• To avoid burns, allow a hot soup mixture to cool slightly before pureeing in a blender.
• To prevent hot soup from curdling when sour cream or yogurt is stirred into it, heat mixture only until it is warm (do not boil).

Favorite Corn Soup

6 medium ears fresh corn
1 large onion, chopped
¼ cup butter or margarine, melted
1 bay leaf
2 whole cloves
Pinch of dried rosemary
Pinch of dried thyme
1½ quarts ready-to-serve chicken broth
Dash of ground nutmeg
Dash of pepper
2 tablespoons cornstarch
1 cup whipping cream
Garnish: fresh parsley sprigs

Cut corn from cob, scraping cob to remove pulp. Set aside.

Cook onion in butter in a Dutch oven until tender. Add 2 cups corn, and cook 3 minutes.

Tie bay leaf, cloves, rosemary, and thyme in a cheesecloth bag. Add cheesecloth bag, chicken broth, nutmeg, and pepper to onion mixture, stirring well. Simmer, uncovered, 45 minutes.

Remove and discard cheesecloth bag. Pour broth mixture through a large wire-mesh strainer into a large container, reserving liquid. Spoon strained vegetables into container of an electric blender; cover and process 30 seconds or until smooth.

Add pureed mixture to strained liquid, and return to Dutch oven. Stir in remaining corn. Bring soup to a boil. Reduce heat, and simmer, uncovered, 10 minutes.

Combine cornstarch and whipping cream; stir into soup. Cook just until thickened. Garnish each serving, if desired. **Yield: 2 quarts.**

Chilled Cucumber-Buttermilk Soup

5 (7- to 8-inch-long) cucumbers (about 2¾ pounds)
½ teaspoon salt
6 green onions, chopped
½ cup chopped fresh parsley
1 tablespoon chopped fresh dill
1 quart buttermilk
1 (16-ounce) carton sour cream
¼ cup lemon juice
¼ teaspoon salt
¼ teaspoon ground white pepper

Peel cucumbers; cut in half lengthwise, and scoop out seeds. Place cucumber shells on a paper towel; sprinkle ½ teaspoon salt evenly over both sides of cucumber. Let stand 30 minutes. Drain; coarsely chop.

Combine cucumber, green onions, and next 7 ingredients. Place one-third of mixture in container of an electric blender; cover and process 1 minute or until smooth. Pour soup into a 3-quart container. Repeat procedure twice with remaining soup. Cover and chill. **Yield: 2¼ quarts.**

Cold Dill Soup

2 cups half-and-half
2 (8-ounce) cartons plain yogurt
2 cucumbers, peeled, seeded, and diced
3 tablespoons minced fresh dill or 1 tablespoon dried dillweed
2 tablespoons lemon juice
1 tablespoon chopped green onions
½ teaspoon salt
⅛ to ¼ teaspoon ground white pepper
Garnishes: cucumber slices, fresh dill sprigs

Combine first 8 ingredients, stirring well; cover and chill thoroughly. Stir well; garnish, if desired. **Yield: 1 quart.**

Creamy Mushroom Soup

4 (10¾-ounce) cans cream of mushroom soup, undiluted
2 cups half-and-half
2 cups milk
1 (8-ounce) carton sour cream
1 (8-ounce) loaf process cheese spread, cubed
⅛ teaspoon red pepper
1 pound fresh mushrooms, sliced
¼ cup dry white wine
Garnish: fresh chives

Combine first 6 ingredients in a large Dutch oven; stir well. Cook over low to medium heat, stirring frequently, until cheese melts.

Stir mushrooms into soup; cook over low heat 20 minutes, stirring frequently. Stir wine into soup just before serving. Garnish, if desired.
Yield: about 3½ quarts.

Creamy Mushroom Soup

Cream of Mustard Greens Soup

Cream of Mustard Greens Soup

1 (1-pound) center-cut ham slice with bone
8 cups water
1 large bunch fresh mustard greens, washed
    and finely chopped (about 4½ cups)
¼ cup butter or margarine
2 cups chopped green onions
2 cups chopped celery
1 cup chopped onion
⅓ cup butter or margarine
⅓ cup all-purpose flour
5 cups half-and-half
½ teaspoon salt
⅛ teaspoon hot sauce

Combine ham and water in a Dutch oven;
bring to a boil. Cover, reduce heat, and simmer 3
hours. Remove ham, leaving liquid in Dutch
oven. (Reserve ham for another use.)

Add mustard greens to Dutch oven, and cook,
uncovered, 1 hour, stirring occasionally. Set aside.

Melt ¼ cup butter in a skillet over medium
heat. Add green onions, celery, and onion; cook,
stirring constantly, until vegetables are tender.
Remove from heat.

Position knife blade in food processor bowl;
add onion mixture. Process onion mixture until
smooth, stopping occasionally to scrape down
sides. Set aside.

Melt ⅓ cup butter in Dutch oven over low
heat; gradually add flour, stirring until smooth.
Cook 1 minute, stirring constantly. Gradually add
half-and-half; cook over medium heat, stirring
constantly, until thickened and bubbly.

Stir in mustard green mixture, pureed vegetables, salt, and hot sauce. Cook just until thoroughly heated (do not boil). **Yield: 2½ quarts.**

Pea and Watercress Soup

3 tablespoons butter or margarine
1 small onion, finely chopped
1 bunch watercress, chopped
½ cup fresh or frozen English peas
2 tablespoons long-grain rice, uncooked
2 cups ready-to-serve chicken broth
1 cup skim milk
¼ teaspoon ground white pepper
Garnish: chopped fresh mint

Melt butter in a large saucepan over medium
heat; add onion, and cook 5 minutes, stirring
constantly. Add watercress; cook 3 minutes, stirring constantly. Add peas and rice; cook 5 minutes, stirring constantly.

Stir in chicken broth; bring to a boil. Cover,
reduce heat, and simmer 20 minutes. Remove
from heat; cool slightly.

Spoon half of mixture into container of an
electric blender; cover and process until smooth.
Pour into a saucepan, and repeat procedure with
remaining mixture.

Stir in milk and white pepper; bring to a boil.
Remove from heat; cool slightly. Cover and chill
thoroughly. Garnish, if desired. **Yield: 2⅓ cups.**

Cream Pea Soup

4 cups shredded lettuce
1 medium onion, chopped
¼ cup butter or margarine, melted
1 tablespoon all-purpose flour
¼ teaspoon ground coriander
2 (10-ounce) packages frozen peas, thawed and divided
3 (14½-ounce) cans ready-to-serve chicken broth
1 cup milk
Cream sherry (optional)
Garnish: fresh mint sprigs

Cook lettuce and onion in butter in a Dutch oven until onion is tender. Add flour and coriander, and cook 1 minute, stirring constantly.

Set aside ¼ cup peas; gradually add broth and remaining peas to Dutch oven. Cover and cook 15 minutes, stirring often.

Place one-fourth of soup mixture in container of an electric blender; cover and process until smooth. Repeat procedure with remaining mixture, returning pureed mixture to Dutch oven.

Stir in milk and reserved ¼ cup peas, and cook until thoroughly heated. If desired, add cream sherry to individual servings, and garnish.
Yield: 2¼ quarts.

From left: Cream Pea Soup and Carrot Cream Soup (page 30)

From left: Black Bean Soup (page 76) and Peanut Butter-Carrot Soup

Peanut Butter-Carrot Soup

1 stalk celery, coarsely chopped
1 medium carrot, coarsely chopped
2 tablespoons chopped onion
¾ cup water
2 chicken-flavored or beef-flavored bouillon
    cubes
2 cups water, divided
½ cup creamy peanut butter
¼ teaspoon pepper
1 tablespoon cornstarch
½ cup half-and-half
Garnishes: carrot strips, chopped peanuts

Combine first 4 ingredients in a saucepan; cover and cook over low heat 10 minutes or until tender. Add bouillon cubes and 1½ cups water; cook, uncovered, until bouillon cubes dissolve.

Pour mixture into container of an electric blender, and add peanut butter and pepper; cover and process until smooth. Return mixture to saucepan.

Combine cornstarch and remaining ½ cup water, stirring until blended; stir into soup mixture. Bring to a boil; reduce heat to low, and cook 1 minute.

Stir in half-and-half; cook over low heat, uncovered, stirring constantly, until thoroughly heated. Ladle into individual soup bowls, and garnish, if desired. **Yield: 3 cups.**

Chilled Sweet Red Pepper Soup

½ cup butter or margarine
3 large sweet red peppers, sliced
2 cups chopped leeks
1½ cups ready-to-serve chicken broth
3 cups buttermilk
⅛ teaspoon ground white pepper
Sweet yellow peppers, halved and seeded
Garnish: fresh chives

Melt butter in a large saucepan. Add sweet red pepper slices, leeks, and chicken broth; bring to a boil. Cover, reduce heat, and simmer, stirring occasionally, 30 minutes or until tender.

Pour mixture into container of an electric blender or food processor; cover and process until smooth, stopping once to scrape down sides.

Pour mixture through a wire-mesh strainer, making sure to get 3 cups liquid. Transfer liquid to a large bowl; stir in buttermilk and ground white pepper.

Cover and chill at least 2 hours. Garnish, if desired. **Yield: 1½ quarts.**

Cream of Roasted Sweet Red Pepper Soup

(pictured on page 27)

8 large sweet red peppers
6 cloves garlic, minced
1 small onion, chopped
3 tablespoons butter or margarine, divided
2 (14½-ounce) cans ready-to-serve chicken broth
2 cups dry white wine
1 bay leaf
½ teaspoon salt
¼ teaspoon pepper
2 tablespoons all-purpose flour
1½ cups whipping cream
Garnish: fresh basil, cut into thin strips

Place peppers on an aluminum foil-lined baking sheet; broil 5½ inches from heat (with electric oven door partially opened) about 5 minutes on each side or until peppers look blistered.

Place roasted peppers in a heavy-duty, zip-top plastic bag immediately; seal and let stand 10 minutes. Peel peppers; remove and discard stem and seeds. Set roasted peppers aside.

Cook garlic and onion in 1 tablespoon melted butter in a Dutch oven over medium heat until crisp-tender. Add chicken broth and next 4 ingredients; bring to a boil. Reduce heat, and simmer 30 minutes.

Pour broth mixture through a large wire-mesh strainer into a large container, reserving solids. Remove bay leaf. Set broth mixture aside.

Position knife blade in food processor bowl; add reserved solids and roasted peppers. Process 30 seconds or until mixture is smooth, stopping once to scrape down sides; set roasted pepper puree aside.

Melt remaining 2 tablespoons butter in Dutch oven over low heat; add flour, stirring until smooth. Cook 1 minute, stirring constantly. Gradually add broth mixture; cook over medium heat, stirring constantly, until thickened and bubbly (about 3 minutes).

Stir in pepper puree. Gradually stir in whipping cream. Cook over low heat until thoroughly heated. Garnish, if desired. **Yield: 2 quarts.**

Freezing Roasted Peppers

Roast extra sweet red and yellow peppers, freeze, and use later to add flavor to soups, pastas, pizzas, and salads. To freeze, cut roasted peppers into strips, and place in a single layer on a baking sheet sprayed with cooking spray. Freeze; remove from baking sheet, and place in a heavy-duty, zip-top plastic bag. Return to the freezer, and use as needed.

Red and Yellow Pepper Soup

Red and Yellow Pepper Soup Techniques

Roast peppers by placing them on a baking sheet and broiling. Turn peppers with tongs as they blister and darken.

Seal roasted peppers in a paper bag for 10 minutes; peel. The captured steam loosens pepper skins, making them easier to peel.

Serve soup by steadily and evenly pouring ½ cup of each pureed pepper mixture into a bowl at the same time.

Red and Yellow Pepper Soup

3 large sweet red peppers
3 large sweet yellow peppers
1½ cups chopped onion
1 tablespoon minced garlic
2 tablespoons olive oil
1 quart ready-to-serve chicken broth, divided
2 tablespoons sherry wine vinegar
Salt and pepper to taste
Garnish: fresh chives

Place peppers on a baking sheet. Broil 5½ inches from heat (with electric oven door partially opened), turning with tongs as peppers blister and turn dark on all sides.

Place peppers in a paper bag; seal and let stand 10 minutes to loosen skins. Peel and discard skins; remove and discard seeds from peppers. Set peppers aside.

Cook onion and garlic in olive oil in a large skillet until onion is tender. Remove from heat.

Combine red peppers, half of onion mixture, and 2 cups chicken broth in container of an electric blender; cover and process until smooth. Transfer mixture to a Dutch oven.

Combine yellow peppers, remaining onion mixture, and remaining 2 cups broth in container of electric blender; cover and process until smooth. Transfer yellow pepper mixture to a separate Dutch oven.

Bring pepper mixtures to a boil; cover, reduce heat, and simmer 10 minutes. Add vinegar and salt and pepper to taste to red pepper mixture; stir well.

Pour steadily and evenly ½ cup of each pepper mixture into individual soup bowls at the same time. Serve warm. Garnish, if desired.
Yield: 1¼ quarts.

Crème Vichyssoise

2 cups coarsely chopped leeks with tops or
    onions
3 cups peeled, sliced potato
3 cups water
4 chicken-flavored bouillon cubes
¼ teaspoon ground white pepper
3 tablespoons butter or margarine
2 cups half-and-half or milk
Garnish: chopped chives

Combine first 6 ingredients in a Dutch oven;
cook over medium heat until tender.

Spoon half of mixture into container of an
electric blender; cover and process until smooth.
Pour into a 2-quart container. Repeat procedure
with remaining mixture.

Stir in half-and-half; cover and chill. Garnish,
if desired. **Yield: 1¼ quarts.**

Velvety Roquefort Vichyssoise

2 cups finely chopped onion
¼ cup butter or margarine, melted
1 quart ready-to-serve chicken broth
2 cups diced potato
¼ teaspoon salt
Pinch of ground white pepper
6 ounces Roquefort cheese, divided
½ cup dry white wine
2 cups buttermilk
2 tablespoons minced fresh parsley

Cook onion in butter in a large Dutch oven
over medium heat 10 minutes or until tender and
slightly golden.

Stir in chicken broth, potato, salt, and pepper;
bring to a boil. Reduce heat; simmer, uncovered,
15 minutes or until potato is tender.

Spoon half of potato mixture into container
of an electric blender; cover and process until

smooth. Repeat with remaining mixture. Return
potato mixture to Dutch oven.

Crumble 4 ounces cheese. Add cheese and
wine to potato mixture; cook over low heat, stirring constantly, about 5 minutes or until cheese
melts. Cool; cover and chill about 4 hours. Stir
in buttermilk. Crumble remaining cheese; sprinkle each serving with cheese and parsley. **Yield:
2 quarts.**

Cucumber Vichyssoise

1 small onion, chopped
2 tablespoons butter or margarine, melted
2 cups ready-to-serve chicken broth
3 medium potatoes, peeled and finely
    chopped
1 teaspoon salt
¼ teaspoon ground white pepper
2 medium cucumbers, peeled, seeded, and
    chopped
2 cups milk
1 cup half-and-half
¼ cup sour cream
Garnish: shreds of cucumber peel

Cook onion in butter in a large saucepan over
medium heat, stirring constantly, until tender.

Add chicken broth and next 3 ingredients.
Bring to a boil; cover, reduce heat, and simmer
12 minutes.

Add chopped cucumber and milk; simmer,
uncovered, 7 minutes.

Stir half-and-half and sour cream into cucumber mixture.

Pour one-third of soup mixture into container
of an electric blender; cover and process until
smooth, stopping once to scrape down sides.
Pour into a large bowl. Repeat procedure twice
with remaining soup mixture.

Cover and chill at least 2 hours. Garnish, if
desired. **Yield: 1¾ quarts.**

Baked Potato Soup

(pictured on cover)

4 large baking potatoes
⅔ cup butter or margarine
⅔ cup all-purpose flour
6 cups milk
¾ teaspoon salt
½ teaspoon pepper
12 slices bacon, cooked, crumbled, and
      divided
4 green onions, chopped and divided
1½ cups (6 ounces) shredded Cheddar cheese,
      divided
1 (8-ounce) carton sour cream

Wash potatoes; prick several times with a fork. Bake at 400° for 1 hour or until done; cool.

Cut potatoes in half lengthwise; scoop out and reserve pulp. Discard shells.

Melt butter in a heavy saucepan over low heat; add flour, stirring until smooth. Cook 1 minute, stirring constantly. Gradually add milk; cook over medium heat, stirring constantly, until thickened and bubbly.

Stir in potato, salt, pepper, ½ cup bacon, 2 tablespoons green onions, and 1 cup cheese. Cook until thoroughly heated (do not boil).

Stir in sour cream; cook just until heated (do not boil). Serve with remaining bacon, green onions, and cheese. **Yield: 2½ quarts.**

Sweet Potato Soup

1 (17-ounce) can sweet potatoes, drained
1 cup orange juice
½ cup white wine
¼ cup honey
¼ cup sour cream
1 teaspoon pumpkin pie spice
Garnish: toasted, flaked coconut

Combine first 6 ingredients in container of an electric blender or food processor; cover and process until smooth.

Chill. Garnish, if desired. **Yield: 3⅓ cups.**

Pumpkin-Pear Soup

3 ripe pears, peeled and thinly sliced
¼ cup chopped onion
2 tablespoons butter, melted
2 cups canned or cooked, mashed pumpkin
2 (14½-ounce) cans ready-to-serve chicken
      broth
½ cup water
¼ cup dry white wine
¼ teaspoon salt
1 (3-inch) stick cinnamon
⅓ cup half-and-half
Garnishes: sour cream, green onion strips

Cook pear and onion in butter in a large skillet over medium-high heat, stirring constantly, until tender. Position knife blade in food processor bowl; add pear mixture and pumpkin. Process until smooth.

Transfer pureed pumpkin mixture to a large saucepan; add chicken broth and next 4 ingredients. Bring to a boil. Reduce heat, and simmer, uncovered, 20 minutes; remove cinnamon stick.

Stir in half-and-half, and heat thoroughly (do not boil). Garnish, if desired. **Yield: 1½ quarts.**

Yellow Squash Soup

Yellow Squash Soup

1 medium onion, finely chopped
2 cloves garlic, minced
1 teaspoon chopped fresh thyme
¼ cup butter or margarine, melted
3 pounds yellow squash, thinly sliced
1 quart ready-to-serve chicken broth
1 cup half-and-half
1 teaspoon salt
Garnishes: edible flowers, fresh thyme sprigs

Cook first 3 ingredients in butter in a large Dutch oven until onion is tender.

Add squash and chicken broth. Bring to a boil; cover, reduce heat, and simmer 20 minutes or until squash is tender.

Transfer mixture in batches to container of an electric blender; cover and process until smooth. Return pureed squash mixture to Dutch oven.

Stir in half-and-half and salt. Cook just until thoroughly heated. Serve hot. Garnish, if desired. **Yield: 2¾ quarts.**

Creamed Butternut and Apple Soup

1 (2½-pound) butternut squash, peeled and diced
¾ pound cooking apples, peeled, cored, and quartered
1 quart ready-to-serve chicken broth
1 (1½-inch) stick cinnamon
1 cup half-and-half
¼ cup unsalted butter or margarine, melted
2 tablespoons maple syrup
¼ teaspoon salt
¼ teaspoon ground nutmeg
¼ teaspoon ground ginger
Garnishes: apple slices, ground nutmeg

Combine first 4 ingredients in a Dutch oven. Bring to a boil; cover, reduce heat, and simmer 20 to 30 minutes or until squash is tender. Remove cinnamon stick.

Spoon mixture into container of an electric blender; cover and process until smooth.

Return squash mixture to Dutch oven; stir in half-and-half and next 5 ingredients. Cook over low heat, stirring constantly, until heated. Serve hot. Garnish, if desired. **Yield: 2 quarts.**

Watercress-Zucchini Soup

3 leeks, sliced (about 2 pounds)
1 tablespoon butter or margarine, melted
1½ pounds zucchini, peeled and sliced
1 quart ready-to-serve chicken broth
1 bunch fresh watercress
⅛ teaspoon pepper
⅓ cup whipping cream

Cook leeks in butter in a Dutch oven 3 minutes. Stir in zucchini, and cook 2 minutes, stirring constantly.

Add chicken broth; bring to a boil, reduce heat, and simmer 4 minutes. Add watercress and pepper; simmer 1 minute.

Spoon one-third of soup mixture into container of an electric blender; cover and process until smooth. Pour into a large bowl. Repeat procedure twice until all mixture is pureed. Add to bowl.

Stir in whipping cream; cover and chill. **Yield: 1¾ quarts.**

Zucchini Soup with Cilantro

1 large onion, chopped
3 tablespoons butter or margarine, melted
3 pounds zucchini, chopped
1 (14½-ounce) can ready-to-serve chicken broth
2 cups buttermilk, divided
1 cup fresh cilantro, chopped and divided
3 tablespoons lemon juice
½ teaspoon salt
¼ to ½ teaspoon pepper
Garnishes: zucchini slices, fresh cilantro sprigs

Cook onion in butter in a 3-quart saucepan over medium heat, stirring constantly, until tender; add zucchini and chicken broth. Bring to a boil; reduce heat, and cook 15 to 20 minutes. Remove from heat; cool.

Combine half of zucchini mixture, ½ cup buttermilk, and ½ cup cilantro in container of an electric blender or food processor; cover and process until smooth, stopping once to scrape down sides. Pour into a large bowl.

Repeat procedure with remaining zucchini mixture, ½ cup buttermilk, and remaining cilantro. Add to bowl, and stir in remaining 1 cup buttermilk, lemon juice, salt, and pepper. Cover and chill at least 8 hours. Garnish each serving, if desired. **Yield: 2 quarts.**

Dried Tomato-Cream Soup

¾ cup dried tomatoes
2 cups water
2 cups whipping cream
½ teaspoon salt
¼ teaspoon freshly ground pepper

Combine tomatoes and water in a large saucepan; bring to a boil, and let boil 2 minutes. Remove from heat, and cool in pan 30 minutes.

Pour mixture into container of an electric blender; cover and process until smooth. Return to saucepan, and stir in remaining ingredients. Cook over low heat until thoroughly heated. Do not boil. **Yield: 3½ cups.**

Tomatillo Soup with Crunchy Jicama

½ pound fresh tomatillos
¼ cup chopped onion
2 tablespoons seeded, chopped poblano pepper
1 tablespoon chopped fresh cilantro or parsley
1 tablespoon lime juice
½ teaspoon salt
½ teaspoon ground cumin
¼ teaspoon sugar
1 clove garlic, minced
1 cup half-and-half
1 cup peeled, finely chopped jicama
Garnishes: tomatillo slices, fresh cilantro sprigs

Remove husks from tomatillos, and rinse. Place tomatillos in a saucepan; add water to cover. Bring to a boil; reduce heat, and simmer 6 minutes or until tender. Drain and cool.

Combine tomatillos, onion, and next 7 ingredients in container of an electric blender or food processor; cover and process until smooth, stopping once to scrape down sides.

Transfer mixture to a large bowl; stir in half-and-half and chopped jicama. Cover and chill. Serve in individual bowls; garnish, if desired. **Yield: 3 cups.**

Tomatillo Soup with Crunchy Jicama

Cantaloupe Soup

8 cups cubed cantaloupe, chilled (about 2
   medium)
¾ cup sweet white wine, chilled
¼ cup whipping cream
Garnish: fresh mint sprigs

Place half of cantaloupe in container of an
electric blender; cover and process until smooth.
With blender running, add half each of wine and
whipping cream; process until smooth.

Repeat procedure with remaining cantaloupe,
wine, and whipping cream. Ladle mixture into
individual soup bowls; garnish, if desired. **Yield:
1½ quarts.**

Peach-Plum Soup

½ pound fresh peaches, peeled and sliced
½ pound fresh plums, peeled and sliced
1 cup plus 2 tablespoons sugar
1 (2-inch) stick cinnamon
1¾ cups water
2 cups dry red wine
1 teaspoon arrowroot
¼ cup water
½ cup whipping cream, whipped

Combine first 6 ingredients in a Dutch oven.
Bring to a boil; reduce heat, and simmer 10 minutes or until fruit is tender.

Spoon 2 cups fruit mixture into container of an
electric blender; cover and process until smooth.
Repeat procedure with remaining mixture.

Return fruit to Dutch oven; bring to a boil.
Combine arrowroot and ¼ cup water; stir into
soup, and boil 1 minute, stirring constantly. Ladle
soup into individual serving bowls. Top each
serving with whipped cream. **Yield: 1½ quarts.**

Strawberry-Banana Soup

2 cups fresh strawberries, sliced
1 small banana, thinly sliced
¼ cup sugar, divided
1 (8-ounce) carton sour cream
1 cup whipping cream
¾ cup milk
¼ cup dry white wine
Garnish: fresh strawberry fans

Combine strawberries, banana, and 2 tablespoons sugar; stir gently, and set aside.

Combine sour cream and remaining 2 tablespoons sugar; add whipping cream, milk, and
wine. Whisk until well blended.

Fold strawberry and banana mixture into sour
cream mixture. Cover and chill 2 hours. Garnish,
if desired. **Yield: 1 quart.**

Sherry-Berry Dessert Soup

2 cups fresh strawberries or raspberries
1 (8-ounce) carton sour cream
1 cup half-and-half
¼ cup sugar
2 tablespoons dry sherry
½ teaspoon vanilla extract
Garnish: fresh mint sprigs

Combine first 6 ingredients in container of an
electric blender; cover and process until smooth,
stopping and scraping sides as necessary.

Pour into individual bowls or wine glasses;
garnish, if desired. **Yield: 3½ cups.**

Rosy Berry Soup

Rosy Berry Soup

2 (10-ounce) packages frozen raspberries or
    strawberries, thawed
2 cups dry red wine
2½ cups water
1 (3-inch) stick cinnamon
¼ cup sugar
2 tablespoons cornstarch
Whipping cream

Combine first 5 ingredients in a stainless steel saucepan (mixture will discolor aluminum). Bring to a boil; reduce heat, and simmer 15 minutes.

Press raspberry mixture through a wire-mesh strainer, reserving ¼ cup. Return liquid to saucepan. Discard seeds.

Combine cornstarch and reserved ¼ cup raspberry liquid; stir until smooth. Bring remaining liquid to a boil. Reduce heat to low, and stir in cornstarch mixture. Cook, stirring constantly, until slightly thickened. Pour into a large bowl.

Cover soup mixture, and chill 6 to 8 hours. Just before serving, ladle into individual serving bowls. Drizzle whipping cream in soup, swirling gently with a knife. **Yield: 1¼ quarts.**

Chilled Strawberry Soup

Chilled Strawberry Soup

5 cups sliced fresh strawberries
2 cups half-and-half
1¼ cups sour cream
¾ cup sifted powdered sugar
¼ cup balsamic vinegar
Garnishes: whipped cream, strawberry slices,
    fresh mint sprigs

Place strawberries in container of an electric blender or food processor; cover and process until smooth.

Transfer puree to a large bowl. Add half-and-half and next 3 ingredients; stir with a wire whisk until smooth. Cover and chill at least 2 hours.

Serve soup in chilled soup bowls. Garnish, if desired. **Yield: 1¾ quarts.**

Cold Fresh Fruit Soup

2 cups coarsely chopped cantaloupe
2½ cups fresh strawberries
¼ cup seedless green grapes
3 cups coarsely chopped cooking apple
¼ cup sugar
2 cups water
¼ cup lemon juice
1¼ cups orange juice
Garnishes: sour cream, orange rind strips

Combine first 7 ingredients in a large Dutch oven; bring to a boil. Reduce heat, and simmer, uncovered, 15 minutes.

Pour half of fruit mixture into container of an electric blender; cover and process until smooth. Repeat procedure with remaining mixture. Stir orange juice into fruit mixture; cover and chill.

Spoon soup into individual serving bowls; garnish, if desired. **Yield: 1¾ quarts.**

Berry-Peach Soup

2 tablespoons cornstarch
1 cup cold water, divided
¾ cup maple-flavored syrup
¾ cup dry white wine
1 teaspoon lemon juice
2 cups sliced fresh peaches, cut into bite-size
    pieces
1 cup sliced strawberries
1 cup fresh blueberries

Combine cornstarch and ¼ cup water in a saucepan; stir until smooth. Add remaining ¾ cup water, syrup, wine, and lemon juice; mix well.

Cook over medium heat, stirring constantly, until mixture comes to a boil. Boil 1 minute. Remove from heat; cool completely.

Stir in fruit; cover soup, and chill thoroughly. **Yield: 1¼ quarts.**

Refreshing Fruit Soup

1 (16-ounce) can applesauce
1 (6-ounce) can unsweetened pineapple juice
1 (8½-ounce) can pear halves, undrained and
    chopped
1 (8-ounce) can pineapple tidbits, undrained
1 cup frozen unsweetened sliced peaches,
    thawed and chopped
2 to 3 tablespoons brandy (optional)
1 teaspoon ground cinnamon
1 cup sliced fresh strawberries

Combine first 7 ingredients in a large bowl; stir gently. Cover and chill several hours.

Stir in strawberries just before serving. **Yield: 1¼ quarts.**

Note: All ingredients may be combined and frozen. Remove from freezer; let stand for 30 minutes. Serve soup while still slushy.

Elegant Chocolate-Apricot Dessert Soup

1 (14½-ounce) can apricot halves in light
    syrup, drained
1 (6-ounce) package semisweet chocolate
    morsels
1 cup milk
1½ cups whipping cream
1 tablespoon apricot-flavored brandy
¼ teaspoon ground cardamom
Whipped cream
Garnish: chocolate strips

Place apricots in container of an electric blender or food processor; cover and process until smooth. Set aside.

Combine chocolate morsels and milk in a deep 2-quart baking dish. Cover with heavy-duty plastic wrap; fold back a small edge of wrap to allow steam to escape. Microwave at MEDIUM HIGH (70% power) 3 to 4 minutes or until chocolate melts. Stir with a wire whisk until mixture is smooth.

Add chocolate mixture to apricot puree in container of electric blender. Add whipping cream, brandy, and cardamom; cover and process until smooth. Cover and chill thoroughly.

Ladle into dessert bowls; top each serving with a dollop of whipped cream, gently swirling with a knife. Garnish, if desired. **Yield: 1 quart.**

Elegant Chocolate-Apricot Dessert Soup

Bisques & Chowders

Stir up a smooth, delicate bisque or a chunky, rich chowder for a satisfying meal-in-a-bowl. Thick with seafood, meat, vegetables, or cheese, these soups offer a tantalizing array of flavors and textures.

Artichoke-Shrimp Bisque, Clam Bisque, Crab and Corn Bisque

Oven-Roasted Vegetable Chowder, Corn Chowder, Mushroom-Potato Chowder

Make-Ahead Tomato-Basil Bisque, Shrimp Bisque, Clam and Sausage Chowder

Chunky Fish Chowder, Creamy Ham Chowder, Harvest Chowder

Mexican Cheddar-Corn Chowder (page 69)

Artichoke-Shrimp Bisque

Artichoke-Shrimp Bisque

2 (10¾-ounce) cans cream of shrimp soup,
    undiluted
3 cups milk
½ (16-ounce) loaf mild Mexican-style process
    cheese spread, cubed
1 (14-ounce) can artichoke hearts, drained
    and chopped
¼ teaspoon seasoned salt
¼ teaspoon ground white pepper
½ teaspoon Beau Monde seasoning (optional)
1 (5-ounce) package frozen cooked small
    shrimp
Garnishes: sweet red pepper slices, fresh
    parsley sprigs

Combine first 7 ingredients in a Dutch oven;
cook over low heat, stirring often, until cheese
melts and mixture is hot.

Add shrimp; cook, stirring often, 1 minute or
until thoroughly heated. Spoon into serving
bowls, and garnish, if desired. **Yield: 2 quarts.**

Note: Bisque may be prepared a day ahead,
except for adding shrimp. When ready to serve,
reheat bisque over low heat, stirring often. Stir in
shrimp as directed above.

Make-Ahead Tomato-Basil Bisque

½ pound leeks, finely chopped
1 stalk celery, chopped
2 to 3 cloves garlic, crushed
2 tablespoons olive oil
2 (14½-ounce) cans Italian plum tomatoes,
    undrained and chopped
12 fresh basil leaves
1 (14½-ounce) can ready-to-serve chicken
    broth
¼ teaspoon salt
¼ teaspoon ground white pepper
1 cup whipping cream
Crème fraîche (optional)

Cook first 3 ingredients in olive oil in a Dutch oven over low heat, stirring constantly, 10 to 12 minutes (do not brown).

Add tomato and basil; cook over medium heat 10 minutes, stirring occasionally.

Add chicken broth, salt, and pepper; bring to a boil. Reduce heat, and simmer, uncovered, 1 hour, stirring occasionally. Cool; cover mixture, and chill 2 hours.

Position knife blade in food processor bowl; add tomato mixture. Process until smooth. (If a finer texture is desired, pour mixture through a fine wire-mesh strainer into a 2-quart container, discarding pulp.) Cover and chill at least 1 hour or overnight.

Stir in whipping cream, and spoon bisque into individual bowls. If desired, pipe crème fraîche on top in a design or initial. **Yield: 1¼ quarts.**

Note: To make your own crème fraîche for the garnish, combine 1 cup sour cream and 1 cup whipping cream.

Clam Bisque

½ cup chopped onion
3 tablespoons butter or margarine, melted
2 tablespoons all-purpose flour
3 (6½-ounce) cans minced clams, undrained
1 (8-ounce) bottle clam juice
1 cup evaporated milk
2 tablespoons tomato juice
1 to 2 tablespoons lemon juice
Garnish: chopped fresh parsley

Cook onion in butter in a heavy saucepan over medium heat, stirring constantly, until tender. Add flour, stirring until smooth. Cook 1 minute, stirring constantly.

Add clams and clam juice; cook over medium heat, stirring constantly, until mixture is bubbly. Reduce heat, and simmer, uncovered, 5 minutes, stirring constantly.

Stir in milk and tomato juice; cook over medium heat, stirring constantly, until mixture is heated. Remove from heat; stir in lemon juice. Garnish, if desired. **Yield: 2 quarts.**

Crab Bisque

1 (10¾-ounce) can cream of mushroom soup,
    undiluted
1 (10¾-ounce) can cream of asparagus soup,
    undiluted
2 cups milk
1 cup half-and-half
1 (6-ounce) can crabmeat, drained and flaked
¼ to ⅓ cup dry white wine or sherry

Combine first 4 ingredients in a saucepan; heat thoroughly, stirring occasionally. Gently stir in crabmeat and wine; heat thoroughly. **Yield: 1½ quarts.**

Crab and Corn Bisque

½ cup chopped celery
½ cup chopped green onions
¼ cup chopped green pepper
½ cup butter or margarine, melted
2 (10¾-ounce) cans cream of potato soup,
    undiluted
1 (17-ounce) can cream-style corn
1½ cups half-and-half
1½ cups milk
2 bay leaves
1 teaspoon dried thyme
½ teaspoon garlic powder
¼ teaspoon ground white pepper
Dash of hot sauce
1 pound fresh lump crabmeat, drained
Garnishes: chopped fresh parsley, lemon slices

Cook first 3 ingredients in butter in a Dutch oven, stirring constantly, until vegetables are tender. Add soup and next 8 ingredients; cook until thoroughly heated.

Stir in crabmeat, and heat thoroughly. Discard bay leaves. Garnish, if desired. **Yield: 2¾ quarts.**

Know Your Soups

Bisque is a thick, creamy soup most often made with chopped or pureed seafood, but it can also contain vegetables or game.

Chowder is a thick, chunky soup rich with seafood, meat, or vegetables. The name chowder comes from the French chaudiere, a large kettle fishermen used when making their soups or stews.

Shrimp Bisque

1¾ pounds unpeeled medium-size fresh shrimp
¼ cup butter or margarine
3 tablespoons all-purpose flour
¼ cup finely chopped celery
¼ cup finely chopped carrot
¼ cup finely chopped onion
1 (10½-ounce) can condensed chicken broth,
    undiluted
1 cup water
¼ teaspoon salt
⅛ to ¼ teaspoon ground red pepper
1½ cups half-and-half
½ cup dry white wine
Garnishes: cooked shrimp with tails, chives

Peel shrimp, and devein, if desired; set aside.

Melt butter in a Dutch oven over medium heat. Add flour, stirring until smooth. Cook 1 minute, stirring constantly. Add celery, carrot, and onion; cook 2 minutes, stirring constantly.

Stir in chicken broth and next 3 ingredients. Bring mixture to a boil over medium heat. Add shrimp, and cook 2 to 3 minutes or until shrimp turn pink. Remove from heat.

Strain shrimp mixture; transfer ⅔ cup liquid to container of an electric blender or food processor, and return remaining liquid to Dutch oven. Set aside 1 cup cooked shrimp.

Add remaining shrimp and cooked vegetables to liquid in blender or food processor; cover and process until smooth.

Return pureed mixture to Dutch oven; heat thoroughly. Stir in half-and-half and 1 cup reserved shrimp. Cook over low heat until thoroughly heated. Stir in wine. Remove from heat.

Ladle bisque into individual serving bowls. Garnish, if desired. **Yield: 1¾ quarts.**

Shrimp Bisque

Seafood Bisque

¾ pound unpeeled medium-size fresh shrimp
¼ cup chopped green onions with tops
¼ cup butter or margarine, melted
¼ cup all-purpose flour
1 quart milk
¼ teaspoon hot sauce
¼ teaspoon salt
¼ teaspoon ground white pepper
¾ cup fresh crabmeat, drained and flaked
3 tablespoons chopped parsley

Peel and chop shrimp; set aside.

Cook green onions in butter in a heavy saucepan over medium heat, stirring constantly, until tender. Add flour, stirring until smooth. Cook 1 minute, stirring constantly.

Add milk gradually; cook over medium heat, stirring constantly, until thickened and bubbly. Stir in hot sauce, salt, and pepper. Stir in crabmeat and shrimp; cook over low heat until shrimp turn pink. Stir in parsley. **Yield: 1¼ quarts.**

Chunky Fish Chowder

½ cup chopped onion
1 clove garlic, minced
2 tablespoons butter or margarine, melted
2 cups water
2 medium potatoes, peeled and diced
1 (10-ounce) package frozen baby lima beans
⅓ cup dry white wine
1 pound cod fillets, cut into 1-inch pieces
1 (16-ounce) can whole tomatoes, drained and chopped
1 (10¾-ounce) can cream of mushroom soup
1 (10-ounce) package frozen whole kernel corn
1 teaspoon lemon-pepper seasoning
1 teaspoon Worcestershire sauce
4 drops of hot sauce
1 cup evaporated skimmed milk

Cook onion and garlic in butter in a Dutch oven over medium heat, stirring constantly, until tender.

Add water and next 3 ingredients. Bring to a boil; cover, reduce heat, and simmer 15 minutes, stirring occasionally.

Add fish and next 6 ingredients; cover and simmer 15 minutes, stirring occasionally. Stir in milk; cook 2 minutes or until thoroughly heated. **Yield: 2 quarts.**

New England Clam Chowder

3 cups water
2 chicken-flavored bouillon cubes
4 medium-size round red potatoes, finely diced
2 (6½-ounce) cans minced clams, undrained
4 slices bacon, cut into 1-inch pieces
¾ cup chopped onion
3 tablespoons butter or margarine
¼ cup plus 2 tablespoons all-purpose flour
1 quart milk
¾ teaspoon salt
¼ teaspoon pepper

Combine water and bouillon cubes in a Dutch oven; bring to a boil. Add potato; cover and simmer 10 minutes or until tender. Drain potato, and set aside. Drain clams, reserving juice. Set clams and juice aside.

Cook bacon and onion in a medium skillet over medium-high heat, stirring constantly, until bacon is crisp and onion is tender. Remove bacon and onion, reserving 2 tablespoons drippings. Set bacon and onion aside.

Combine reserved drippings and butter in Dutch oven; cook over low heat until butter melts. Add flour, stirring until smooth. Cook, stirring constantly, 1 minute.

Add reserved clam juice and milk gradually; cook over medium heat, stirring constantly, until mixture is thickened and bubbly. Remove mixture from heat; stir in potato, clams, bacon mixture, salt, and pepper. Cook, stirring constantly, until mixture is thoroughly heated (do not boil). **Yield: 2 quarts.**

Clam Chowder

4 slices bacon, chopped
3 (6⅓-ounce) cans whole shelled clams
3 tablespoons butter or margarine
½ cup chopped celery
½ cup chopped onion
2 green onions with tops, chopped
2 cups chopped potato
3 tablespoons all-purpose flour
2 cups milk
2 cups half-and-half
¼ teaspoon hot sauce
½ teaspoon salt
¼ teaspoon ground white pepper
Paprika
Garnish: fresh parsley sprigs

Cook bacon in a Dutch oven until crisp; pour off pan drippings. Set aside.

Drain clams, reserving 1 cup juice; set clams aside. Add clam juice, butter, and next 4 ingredients to bacon in Dutch oven. Bring to a boil; cover, reduce heat, and simmer 15 minutes or until potato is tender.

Chop clams coarsely; set aside.

Combine flour and milk; stir until smooth. Add milk mixture, clams, half-and-half, hot sauce, salt, and pepper to Dutch oven. Cook over medium heat, stirring constantly, until chowder is thoroughly heated.

Sprinkle each serving with paprika, and garnish, if desired. **Yield: 2 quarts.**

Clam and Sausage Chowder

2 dozen fresh clams
2 pounds smoked Polish sausage, thinly sliced
1 medium onion, chopped
2 cloves garlic, minced
2 tablespoons olive oil
1½ pounds potatoes, cubed
1 (10-ounce) package frozen whole kernel corn, thawed
4 (8-ounce) bottles clam juice
2 cups water
1 teaspoon fennel seeds, crushed
½ to 1 teaspoon ground red pepper
2 (16-ounce) cans crushed tomatoes, undrained
½ cup fresh parsley, chopped

Wash clams thoroughly, discarding any opened shells; set aside.

Brown sausage in a Dutch oven over medium heat; drain on paper towels, and set aside.

Cook onion and garlic in olive oil in a Dutch oven over medium-high heat, stirring constantly, until tender. Add potato and next 5 ingredients.

Bring to a boil; cover, reduce heat, and simmer 15 minutes or until potato is tender. Stir in tomatoes.

Remove 2 cups potato mixture, and pour into container of an electric blender. Cover and process until smooth, stopping once to scrape down sides. Return mixture to Dutch oven.

Bring to a boil. Add clams; cover, reduce heat, and simmer 4 to 5 minutes or until clam shells open. (Discard any unopened shells.)

Stir in sausage and parsley; cook until thoroughly heated. **Yield: 3 quarts.**

Manhattan-Style Seafood Chowder

Manhattan-Style Seafood Chowder

4 medium onions, chopped
1 large green pepper, seeded and chopped
¼ cup vegetable oil
2 tablespoons all-purpose flour
3 (14½-ounce) cans stewed tomatoes, undrained
1 tablespoon celery salt
1 teaspoon garlic powder
1 teaspoon hot sauce
½ teaspoon pepper
2 pounds unpeeled medium-size fresh shrimp
½ pound fresh crabmeat, drained and flaked
½ pound firm white fish fillets, cut into bite-size pieces
1 (12-ounce) container Standard oysters, drained
Garnish: celery leaves

Cook onion and green pepper in oil in a Dutch oven over medium-high heat, stirring constantly, until tender.

Add flour; cook, stirring constantly, 1 minute. Stir in tomatoes and next 4 ingredients. Bring to a boil; cover, reduce heat, and simmer 15 minutes.

Peel shrimp. Add shrimp, crabmeat, fish, and oysters to Dutch oven; cover and simmer 15 minutes. Garnish, if desired. **Yield: 3 quarts.**

Curried Seafood Chowder

1 pound unpeeled medium-size fresh shrimp
3 tablespoons butter or margarine
3 tablespoons all-purpose flour
1 tablespoon curry powder
2 cups ready-to-serve chicken broth
2 (8-ounce) bottles clam juice
2 cups half-and-half
4 medium potatoes, peeled and chopped
1 pound grouper or amberjack fillets, cut into bite-size pieces

Peel shrimp, and devein, if desired; set aside.

Melt butter in a large Dutch oven over medium heat; add flour and curry powder, stirring constantly, until smooth. Cook 1 minute, stirring constantly. Gradually add chicken broth, stirring until smooth.

Stir in clam juice, half-and-half, and potato. Bring to a boil; reduce heat, and simmer 20 minutes or until potato is tender.

Add fish and shrimp; cook 5 minutes or until shrimp turn pink. Serve chowder immediately. **Yield: 3½ quarts.**

Shrimp Chowder

8 slices bacon
1 medium onion, chopped
1 stalk celery, chopped
1 green pepper, seeded and chopped
2 (10¾-ounce) cans cream of potato soup, undiluted
1 (10¾-ounce) can cream of celery soup, undiluted
2 (4¼-ounce) cans small shrimp, drained and rinsed
1 quart milk
¼ teaspoon pepper

Cook bacon in a large Dutch oven until crisp; remove bacon, reserving 1 tablespoon drippings in Dutch oven. Crumble bacon, and set aside.

Cook onion, celery, and green pepper in bacon drippings over medium heat, stirring constantly, until tender.

Add potato soup and next 4 ingredients, stirring well. Cook over medium heat until thoroughly heated. Sprinkle each serving with bacon. **Yield: 2½ quarts.**

Chicken Chowder Sauterne

1 (3½- to 4-pound) broiler-fryer, cut up and
   skinned
1 quart water
1 large carrot, scraped and sliced
1 teaspoon salt
1 cup milk
½ cup chopped green onions
½ cup chopped green pepper
½ cup chopped fresh parsley
½ cup chopped celery
2 tablespoons butter or margarine, melted
3 tablespoons butter or margarine
⅓ cup all-purpose flour
1 egg yolk, beaten
½ cup Sauterne
½ teaspoon salt
¼ teaspoon pepper

Combine first 4 ingredients in a large Dutch
oven; bring to a boil. Cover, reduce heat, and
simmer 35 minutes or until chicken is tender.

Drain chicken, reserving broth. Cool, bone,
and chop chicken; set aside. Strain broth, reserving 3 cups. Add milk to reserved broth; set aside.

Cook green onions and next 3 ingredients in 2
tablespoons butter in a heavy skillet over medium
heat, stirring constantly, until tender; set aside.

Melt 3 tablespoons butter in a heavy Dutch
oven over low heat; add flour, stirring well. Cook
1 minute, stirring constantly.

Add reserved broth mixture gradually; cook
over medium heat, stirring constantly, until thickened and bubbly.

Combine egg yolk and wine; mix well. Stir
into broth mixture. Add chicken, vegetables, ½
teaspoon salt, and pepper; cook, stirring constantly, until thoroughly heated. **Yield: 2 quarts.**

Crowd-Pleasing Turkey Chowder

1 turkey carcass
4 quarts water
1 cup butter or margarine
1 cup all-purpose flour
3 onions, chopped
2 large carrots, diced
2 stalks celery, diced
1 cup long-grain rice, uncooked
2 teaspoons salt
¾ teaspoon pepper
2 cups half-and-half
Garnish: fresh parsley sprigs

Place turkey carcass and water in a large
Dutch oven; bring to a boil. Cover, reduce heat,
and simmer 1 hour.

Remove carcass from broth, and pick meat
from bones. Set meat aside. Measure broth, and
add water, if necessary, to measure 3 quarts; set
broth aside.

Melt butter in Dutch oven; add flour, and cook
over medium heat, stirring constantly, 5 minutes.
(Roux will be a very light color.)

Stir onion, carrot, and celery into roux; cook
over medium heat 10 minutes, stirring often.

Add broth, turkey, rice, salt, and pepper; bring
to a boil. Cover, reduce heat, and simmer 20 minutes or until rice is tender. Add half-and-half, and
cook until thoroughly heated. Garnish, if desired.
Yield: 4½ quarts.

Crowd-Pleasing Turkey Chowder

Turkey Chowder

2 tablespoons butter or margarine
2 tablespoons all-purpose flour
2 cups milk
2 cups cubed process cheese
2 cups chopped cooked turkey
1½ cups sliced cooked potato
1 (10-ounce) package frozen mixed vegetables
1 teaspoon chicken-flavored bouillon granules
½ teaspoon instant minced onion
¼ teaspoon dry mustard
⅛ teaspoon pepper

Melt butter in a large saucepan over low heat; add flour, stirring until smooth. Cook 1 minute, stirring constantly.

Add milk and cheese gradually; cook over medium heat, stirring constantly, until mixture thickens and cheese melts.

Add turkey and remaining ingredients, and mix well. Cook over low heat, stirring occasionally, until vegetables are tender. **Yield: 1¼ quarts.**

Creamy Ham Chowder

1 (8-ounce) package frozen mixed vegetables
1 (18¾-ounce) can creamy chunky mushroom soup, undiluted
1 cup milk
¼ teaspoon dried dillweed
⅛ teaspoon coarsely ground black pepper
1 (6¾-ounce) can chunk ham, drained and broken into chunks
¼ cup (1 ounce) shredded Swiss cheese
¼ to ½ cup plain croutons

Place vegetables in a 2-quart baking dish. Cover tightly with heavy-duty plastic wrap; fold back a small edge of wrap to allow steam to escape. Microwave at HIGH 7 to 9 minutes or until vegetables are crisp-tender.

Uncover and stir in soup; gradually add milk, stirring until blended. Add dillweed and pepper. Microwave at HIGH 3 minutes; stir.

Add ham, and microwave at HIGH 2 to 3 minutes or until thoroughly heated. Let stand 2 minutes. Sprinkle each serving with shredded cheese and croutons. **Yield: 1 quart.**

Sausage-Bean Chowder

2 pounds ground pork sausage
4 cups water
2 (16-ounce) cans kidney beans, undrained
2 (16-ounce) cans whole tomatoes, undrained and chopped
2 medium onions, chopped
2 medium potatoes, peeled and cubed
½ cup chopped green pepper
1 large bay leaf
½ teaspoon salt
½ teaspoon dried thyme
¼ teaspoon garlic powder
¼ teaspoon pepper

Brown sausage in a Dutch oven, stirring until it crumbles; drain off drippings.

Add water and remaining ingredients to Dutch oven; bring to a boil. Cover, reduce heat, and simmer 1 hour. Remove bay leaf before serving. **Yield: 3 quarts.**

Simmering Success

An enameled cast-iron Dutch oven is excellent for cooking bisques and chowders because it allows steady simmering with little risk of scorching. Heavy stainless steel and aluminum pots are also good choices.

Fresh Corn and Bacon Chowder

8 ears fresh corn
4 slices bacon
½ cup finely chopped onion
½ cup thinly sliced celery
1 cup water
2 cups milk, divided
1 teaspoon sugar
1 teaspoon dried thyme
½ teaspoon salt
¼ teaspoon pepper
2 teaspoons cornstarch

Cut off tips of corn kernels into a large bowl; scrape milk and remaining pulp from cob with a paring knife. Set aside.

Cook bacon in a large Dutch oven until crisp; remove bacon, reserving 2 tablespoons drippings in Dutch oven. Crumble bacon, and set aside.

Cook onion and celery in reserved bacon drippings over medium-high heat, stirring constantly, until tender.

Stir in corn and water. Bring to a boil; cover, reduce heat, and simmer 10 minutes, stirring occasionally. Stir in 1½ cups milk and next 4 ingredients.

Combine cornstarch and remaining ½ cup milk; stir until smooth. Gradually add to corn mixture, stirring constantly. Cover and cook 10 minutes, stirring often, until thickened and bubbly. Sprinkle with bacon. **Yield: 1¼ quarts.**

Fresh Corn and Bacon Chowder

Hot Cheese Chowder

½ cup chopped celery
½ cup chopped onion
½ cup chopped green pepper
¼ cup butter or margarine, melted
3 cups chicken broth
1 medium potato, peeled and cubed
½ cup chopped carrot
½ cup all-purpose flour
2 cups milk, divided
12 ounces sharp American cheese, cubed
1 tablespoon chopped fresh parsley

Cook celery, onion, and green pepper in butter in a Dutch oven, stirring constantly, until tender.

Add chicken broth, potato, and carrot; bring to a boil. Cover, reduce heat, and simmer 20 minutes or until vegetables are tender.

Combine flour and ¾ cup milk; stir until smooth. Stir flour mixture, remaining 1¼ cups milk, cheese, and parsley into vegetable mixture. Cook over low heat, stirring constantly, until chowder is thickened and bubbly. Serve immediately. **Yield: 2 quarts.**

Harvest Chowder

4 slices bacon
2 stalks celery, thinly sliced
2 carrots, thinly sliced
2 green onions, sliced
2 cups mashed potatoes
1 (17-ounce) can cream-style corn
½ cup frozen English peas
2 cups milk
½ teaspoon salt
1 cup (4 ounces) shredded sharp Cheddar
    cheese
1 large tomato, peeled and thinly sliced
Seasoned pepper

Cook bacon in a large saucepan until crisp; remove bacon, reserving 1 tablespoon drippings in pan. Crumble bacon, and set aside.

Cook celery, carrot, and green onions in drippings 5 to 8 minutes, stirring constantly. Stir in potatoes and next 5 ingredients. Cook over medium heat, stirring constantly, until cheese melts.

Ladle into individual serving bowls. Top each with a tomato slice, bacon, and a dash of seasoned pepper. **Yield: about 1¾ quarts.**

Corn Chowder

1 cup chopped onion
½ cup chopped celery
2 tablespoons butter or margarine, melted
3 cups fresh corn, cut from cob
1½ cups peeled, cubed potato
1½ cups water
2 chicken-flavored bouillon cubes
1 teaspoon salt
¼ teaspoon pepper
¼ teaspoon dried thyme
2 cups milk
1 cup half-and-half

Cook onion and celery in butter in a large saucepan, stirring constantly, until tender. Stir in corn and next 6 ingredients; cover and simmer 15 minutes.

Add milk and half-and-half; cook chowder, stirring constantly, until thoroughly heated. **Yield: 2 quarts.**

Note: You may substitute 3 cups frozen corn for fresh.

Pepper-Cheese Chowder

Pepper-Cheese Chowder

1 cup chopped sweet red pepper
1 cup chopped sweet yellow pepper
½ cup chopped carrot
½ cup sliced celery
½ cup chopped onion
2 cloves garlic, minced
⅓ cup butter or margarine, melted
½ cup all-purpose flour
1 quart half-and-half
2 (10½-ounce) cans condensed chicken broth
1 (12-ounce) can beer
½ teaspoon dry mustard
¼ teaspoon dried rosemary, crushed
¼ teaspoon salt
¼ teaspoon ground red pepper
½ teaspoon freshly ground black pepper
2 cups (8 ounces) shredded sharp Cheddar
    cheese
Garnishes: fresh rosemary sprigs, finely
    chopped sweet red and yellow pepper

Cook first 6 ingredients in butter in a large Dutch oven over medium-high heat, stirring constantly, 5 minutes or until tender.

Add flour, stirring constantly. Cook 1 minute, stirring constantly. Gradually add half-and-half, chicken broth, and beer; cook, stirring constantly, until thickened and bubbly.

Stir in mustard and next 4 ingredients; gradually add cheese, stirring until cheese melts. Ladle into individual serving bowls; garnish, if desired. Serve chowder immediately. **Yield: 2¾ quarts.**

Tortilla-Corn Chowder

Tortilla-Corn Chowder

5 cups ready-to-serve chicken broth
1 large onion, chopped
2 cloves garlic, minced
6 large ears fresh corn
4 (6-inch) corn tortillas, coarsely chopped
1 (4.5 ounce) can chopped green chiles,
      undrained
½ cup sour cream
2 to 3 tablespoons chopped fresh cilantro
¼ teaspoon salt
¼ teaspoon pepper
Garnishes: crushed tortilla chips, sour cream,
      fresh cilantro sprigs

Combine first 3 ingredients in a Dutch oven. Cut corn from cobs, scraping cobs well to remove all milk; add corn to Dutch oven.

Stir in tortilla pieces. Cover and simmer over medium-low heat 1 hour and 15 minutes, stirring occasionally. Remove from heat.

Stir in green chiles and next 4 ingredients; cook until heated. Spoon into individual soup bowls. Garnish, if desired. **Yield: 2 quarts.**

Variation

Cream of Corn Soup: Transfer simmered corn-tortilla mixture to container of an electric blender; cover and process until smooth. Return mixture to Dutch oven. Stir in green chiles and next 4 ingredients; proceed as directed above.

Mexican Cheddar-Corn Chowder

(pictured on page 53)

1 tablespoon butter or margarine
½ cup chopped onion
2 cups peeled and diced potato
1 cup water
½ teaspoon dried basil
2 cups milk
2 (17-ounce) cans cream-style corn
1 (14½-ounce) can whole tomatoes, drained
      and chopped
1 (4.5 ounce) can chopped green chiles,
      undrained
½ cup diced sweet red pepper
½ teaspoon salt
⅛ teaspoon pepper
1 cup (4 ounces) shredded sharp Cheddar
      cheese

Place butter in a deep 3-quart baking dish; microwave, uncovered, at HIGH 35 seconds or until melted. Stir in chopped onion; microwave, uncovered, at HIGH 3 to 4 minutes or until onion is tender.

Add potato, water, and basil. Cover with heavy-duty plastic wrap; fold back a small edge of wrap to allow steam to escape. Microwave at HIGH 12 to 15 minutes or until potato is tender, stirring every 5 minutes.

Stir in milk and next 6 ingredients; cover and microwave at HIGH 5 to 6 minutes or until thoroughly heated, stirring after 3 minutes.

Stir in cheese; reduce to MEDIUM LOW (30% power). Cover and microwave 5 to 6 minutes or until cheese melts, stirring after 3 minutes. Serve immediately. **Yield: 2½ quarts.**

Mushroom-Potato Chowder

1 small onion, chopped
1 stalk celery, chopped
½ small green pepper, seeded and chopped
1 (8-ounce) package sliced fresh mushrooms
2 tablespoons butter or margarine, melted
2 cups peeled and diced red potato
2 cups ready-to-serve chicken broth
½ teaspoon dried thyme or 1½ teaspoons
    minced fresh thyme
2 cups milk, divided
½ teaspoon salt
½ teaspoon pepper
3 tablespoons all-purpose flour
Garnish: fresh thyme sprigs

Cook first 4 ingredients in butter in a large Dutch oven over medium heat, stirring constantly, until tender.

Stir in potato, chicken broth, and thyme. Bring to a boil; reduce heat, and simmer, uncovered, 30 minutes or until potato is tender.

Stir in 1½ cups milk, salt, and pepper. Combine flour and remaining ½ cup milk, stirring until smooth. Stir into chowder, and simmer, uncovered, stirring frequently, until slightly thickened. Garnish, if desired. **Yield: 1½ quarts.**

Mushroom-Potato Chowder

Vegetable-Cheddar Chowder

3 cups water
3 chicken-flavored bouillon cubes
4 medium potatoes, peeled and diced
1 medium onion, sliced
1 cup thinly sliced carrot
½ cup diced green pepper
⅓ cup butter or margarine
⅓ cup all-purpose flour
3½ cups milk
4 cups (16 ounces) shredded sharp Cheddar
  cheese
1 (2-ounce) jar diced pimiento, drained
¼ teaspoon hot sauce (optional)
Garnish: fresh parsley sprigs

Combine water and bouillon cubes in a Dutch oven; bring to a boil. Add vegetables; cover and simmer 12 minutes or until vegetables are tender.

Melt butter in a heavy saucepan over low heat; add flour, stirring until smooth. Cook 1 minute, stirring constantly.

Add milk gradually; cook over medium heat, stirring constantly, until thickened and bubbly. Add cheese, stirring until melted.

Stir cheese sauce, pimiento, and hot sauce, if desired, into vegetable mixture. Cook over low heat until thoroughly heated (do not boil). Garnish each serving, if desired. **Yield: 2½ quarts.**

Oven-Roasted Vegetable Chowder

1½ pounds red potatoes, cut into ½-inch
  cubes
2 large carrots, scraped and cut into ½-inch
  cubes
1 large onion, coarsely chopped
6 plum tomatoes, quartered lengthwise
3 (14½-ounce) cans ready-to-serve chicken
  broth
Dash of salt (optional)
Dash of pepper (optional)

Combine potato and carrot in a lightly greased foil-lined 13- x 9- x 2-inch pan. Bake at 375° for 15 minutes.

Stir in onion. Place tomato at one end of pan, keeping separate from potato mixture. Bake 1 hour, stirring every 15 minutes.

Remove vegetables from oven. Coarsely chop tomato; set aside.

Bring chicken broth to a boil in a large saucepan; add potato mixture. Reduce heat, and simmer 10 to 15 minutes.

Stir in tomato; if desired, add salt and pepper. Serve immediately. **Yield: about 1¾ quarts.**

Keep Garnishes Simple

A garnish should complement the flavors in a soup. Try these for added flavor and texture:
• Thinly sliced carrot or green onions
• Shredded cheese or toasted nuts
• Chopped fresh herbs or sprigs of fresh herbs
• Dollops of sour cream, yogurt, or whipped cream
• Croutons, corn chips, or crackers
• Chopped hard-cooked egg or cooked, crumbled bacon
• Lemon or lime slices or strips of citrus rind

Hearty Vegetable Chowder

Hearty Vegetable Chowder

1 (10½-ounce) can condensed chicken broth,
    undiluted
⅔ cup water
4 cups frozen mixed vegetables
¼ cup chopped onion
¼ cup green pepper, seeded and chopped
3 tablespoons butter or margarine, melted
¼ cup all-purpose flour
½ teaspoon paprika
½ teaspoon dry mustard
2 cups milk
⅛ teaspoon pepper
2 cups (8 ounces) shredded Cheddar cheese
Garnishes: carrot curls, fresh parsley sprigs

Combine chicken broth and water in a saucepan; bring to a boil. Add mixed vegetables, and cook over medium heat 15 minutes or until vegetables are tender.

Cook onion and green pepper in butter in a Dutch oven, stirring constantly, until tender. Stir in flour, paprika, and mustard.

Add milk, vegetables, and broth to Dutch oven; cook over medium heat, stirring constantly, until mixture comes to a boil.

Remove from heat; add pepper and cheese, and stir until cheese melts. Garnish, if desired.
Yield: 1¾ quarts.

Hearty Soups

Chock-full of vegetables, meat, or seafood, these soups stand on their own as main dishes. Pair them with a green salad or crusty bread, and you'll have a substantial meal.

Garden Festival Soup, Black Bean Soup, Spicy Three-Bean Soup

Taco Soup, Beefy Lentil Soup, Italian Spinach Soup with Meatballs, Steak Soup

Chunky Minestrone, French Market Soup Mix, Sausage, Bacon, and Bean Soup

Southern Bouillabaisse, Bean 'n' Ham Soup, Ground Beef Soup

Guadalajara Soup (page 84)

Garden Festival Soup

Garden Festival Soup

3 cups water
1 cup peeled, diced red potato
1 cup scraped, sliced carrot
1½ teaspoons salt
1 (16-ounce) package frozen English peas, thawed
1½ cups broccoli flowerets
1 cup cauliflower flowerets
1 cup sliced yellow squash
¼ cup chopped green onions
¼ cup butter or margarine, melted
¼ cup all-purpose flour
2 cups milk
2 cups half-and-half
1 (2-ounce) jar diced pimiento, drained
¼ teaspoon ground white pepper
3 dashes of hot sauce
Garnish: chopped fresh parsley

Combine first 4 ingredients in a large sauce-pan; stir well. Bring to a boil; cover, reduce heat, and simmer 10 minutes.

Stir in peas and next 3 ingredients; cover and simmer 10 minutes or until vegetables are tender. Remove from heat, and set aside.

Cook chopped green onions in butter in a large Dutch oven over medium heat, stirring constantly, until tender.

Add flour, stirring until smooth. Cook 1 minute, stirring constantly. Gradually add milk and half-and-half; cook over medium heat, stirring constantly, until mixture is thickened and bubbly.

Add pimiento, pepper, and hot sauce; stir well. Gradually add reserved vegetables and liquid, stirring well. Cook mixture, uncovered, over medium heat until thoroughly heated, stirring occasionally.

Ladle soup into individual serving bowls. Garnish, if desired. Serve soup immediately. **Yield: 2¼ quarts.**

Garden Vegetable Soup

1 cup thinly sliced carrot
1 cup sliced celery with leaves
1 cup chopped onion
1 clove garlic, crushed
¼ cup butter or margarine, melted
9 medium tomatoes, peeled and chopped
1 teaspoon dried oregano
1 teaspoon dried basil
2 teaspoons salt
¼ teaspoon pepper
1 (14½-ounce) can ready-to-serve beef broth
⅓ pound fresh green beans, washed and cut into 1-inch pieces
1 medium zucchini, halved lengthwise and sliced
¼ cup chopped fresh parsley
Grated Parmesan cheese (optional)

Cook first 4 ingredients in butter in a large Dutch oven over medium heat, stirring constantly, until onion is tender.

Add tomato and seasonings; bring to a boil. Reduce heat and simmer 15 minutes, stirring occasionally.

Add beef broth and green beans; simmer 20 minutes. Add zucchini and parsley; simmer 10 minutes. Spoon into soup bowls; sprinkle with Parmesan cheese, if desired. **Yield: 2¼ quarts.**

Vegetable Variety

When adding vegetables to home-made soup, remember that not all vegetables cook in the same length of time. Those that take the longest to cook should be cut into uniform pieces and added first. Add frozen vegetables after fresh. Canned vegetables need only to be reheated.

Black Bean Soup

(pictured on page 38)

1 (16-ounce) package dried black beans
7 cups water
2 (14½-ounce) cans ready-to-serve chicken broth
1 small ham hock
1 tablespoon butter or margarine
2 cloves garlic, crushed
1 small hot pepper, chopped
1 medium onion, chopped
1 stalk celery, chopped
1 bay leaf
½ teaspoon salt
½ teaspoon pepper
½ teaspoon dry mustard
¼ cup dry sherry
Feta cheese (optional)

Sort and wash beans; place in a Dutch oven. Add 7 cups water. Bring to a boil; cover beans, and cook 2 minutes. Remove from heat, and let stand 1 hour.

Add chicken broth and next 10 ingredients to beans. Bring to a boil; cover, reduce heat, and simmer 2 to 2½ hours, stirring occasionally. Remove bay leaf.

Remove ham hock; cut off meat, and dice. Discard bone, and set meat aside.

Measure 4 cups soup, and pour into container of an electric blender; cover and process until smooth. Return mixture to Dutch oven.

Add diced ham and sherry. Bring mixture to a boil; reduce heat, and simmer soup 10 minutes. Sprinkle each serving with feta cheese, if desired. **Yield: 2¼ quarts.**

Note: Seeds in small hot pepper make soup very hot. For a milder soup, remove seeds before chopping pepper.

Three-Bean Soup

2 cups dried navy beans
1 cup dried red beans
1½ cups dried garbanzo beans
3 (10½-ounce) cans condensed chicken broth, undiluted
3⅔ cups water
2 onions, chopped
1 cup sliced carrot
1 cup sliced celery
1 large clove garlic, minced
2 tablespoons parsley flakes
2 teaspoons dried basil
1 teaspoon dried oregano
1 teaspoon salt
½ teaspoon pepper
3 cups chopped fresh spinach (about 4 ounces)
Grated Parmesan cheese (optional)

Sort and wash beans; place in a large Dutch oven. Cover with water 2 inches above beans; let soak 8 hours.

Drain beans, and return to Dutch oven. Add chicken broth and next 10 ingredients. Bring to a boil; cover, reduce heat, and simmer 2 hours or until beans are tender, stirring occasionally.

Add spinach, and cook 10 to 15 minutes, stirring occasionally. Sprinkle each serving with Parmesan cheese, if desired. **Yield: 3 quarts.**

Three-Bean Soup

French Market Soup Mix

1 pound dried black beans
1 pound dried Great Northern beans
1 pound dried navy beans
1 pound dried pinto beans
1 pound dried red beans
1 pound dried black-eyed peas
1 pound dried green split peas
1 pound dried yellow split peas
1 pound dried lentils
1 pound dried baby limas
1 pound dried large limas
1 pound barley pearls

Combine all ingredients in a very large bowl. Divide mixture into 13 (2-cup) packages to give along with the recipe for French Market Soup. **Yield: 26 cups.**

French Market Soup

1 (2-cup) package French Market Soup Mix
2 quarts water
1 large ham hock
1 (16-ounce) can whole tomatoes, undrained and coarsely chopped
1½ cups chopped onion
3 tablespoons lemon juice
1 chile pepper, coarsely chopped
1 clove garlic, minced
1¼ teaspoons salt
¼ teaspoon pepper

Sort and wash soup mix; place in a Dutch oven. Cover with water 2 inches above soup mix; let soak 8 hours.

Drain soup mix, and return to Dutch oven; add 2 quarts water and ham hock. Bring to a boil; cover, reduce heat, and simmer 1½ hours or until beans are tender.

Stir in tomato and next 4 ingredients. Bring mixture to a boil, reduce heat, and simmer, uncovered, 30 minutes.

Remove ham hock; remove meat from bone. Chop meat, and return to soup. Stir in salt and pepper. **Yield: 3 quarts.**

Black, White, and Red All Over Soup

1 (15.5-ounce) can white hominy, drained and rinsed
1 (15-ounce) can black beans, drained and rinsed
1 (14½-ounce) can chili-style diced tomatoes, undrained
1 (14½-ounce) can ready-to-serve chicken broth
1 teaspoon chopped fresh cilantro
½ teaspoon chili powder
½ teaspoon ground cumin

Combine all ingredients in a large saucepan; cook over medium heat, stirring occasionally, until thoroughly heated. **Yield: 1¼ quarts.**

Soaking Dried Beans

Dried beans require soaking to rehydrate.

For **quick soaking**, add 6 to 8 cups water to 1 pound dried beans. Bring to a boil; cover and cook 2 minutes. Remove from heat, and let stand 1 hour.

For **overnight soaking**, add 6 cups water to 1 pound dried beans. Let stand 8 hours at room temperature. (Beans tend to sour if they are placed in too warm a place.) Beans soaked using this method retain their shape and cook faster.

Chunky Minestrone

Chunky Minestrone

1 large onion, chopped
1 medium carrot, halved lengthwise and sliced
  (about ¾ cup)
1 clove garlic, minced
1 tablespoon olive oil
½ cup long-grain rice, uncooked
2½ cups water
2 (14½-ounce) cans Italian-style stewed
  tomatoes, undrained and chopped
1 (10½-ounce) can condensed chicken broth,
  undiluted
1⅓ cups water
2 teaspoons dried Italian seasoning
½ teaspoon salt
¼ teaspoon pepper
1 medium zucchini, halved lengthwise and
  sliced
1 (15-ounce) can cannellini beans, undrained
1 (10-ounce) package frozen chopped spinach,
  thawed
⅔ cup grated Parmesan cheese

Cook first 3 ingredients in oil in a large Dutch oven over medium-high heat 3 minutes, stirring constantly.

Add rice and next 7 ingredients. Bring to a boil. Cover, reduce heat, and simmer 20 minutes.

Add zucchini, beans, and spinach; cook 5 additional minutes. Sprinkle each serving with cheese. **Yield: 2 quarts.**

Split Pea Soup

1 (16-ounce) package dried green split peas
2 quarts water
1 medium onion, chopped
1 medium carrot, diced
1 stalk celery, diced
1 meaty ham bone
¼ to ½ teaspoon salt
¼ teaspoon pepper
¼ teaspoon dried tarragon

Sort and wash peas; place in a Dutch oven. Add 2 quarts water, and bring to a boil. Cover and cook 2 minutes. Remove from heat, and let stand 1 hour.

Add vegetables, ham bone, and seasonings. Bring to a boil; cover, reduce heat, and simmer 2½ to 3 hours, stirring occasionally.

Remove bone; cut off meat, and dice. Discard bone. Return meat to soup, and simmer 10 additional minutes. **Yield: 2 quarts.**

Bean 'n' Ham Soup

Bean 'n' Ham Soup

1 pound dried Great Northern beans
1 quart water
1 (10½-ounce) can beef consommé, undiluted
1 meaty ham hock
6 black peppercorns
3 cloves garlic, halved
2 bay leaves
2 fresh parsley sprigs
2 fresh thyme sprigs
1 cup water
3 large carrots, scraped and sliced
2 cups coarsely chopped cooked ham
1 small onion, finely chopped
4 medium potatoes, peeled and cubed
Dash of hot sauce
Salt and freshly ground pepper to taste

Sort and wash beans; place in a Dutch oven. Cover with water 2 inches above beans; let soak 8 hours.

Drain beans, and return to Dutch oven. Add 1 quart water, consommé, and ham hock; bring to a boil. Place peppercorns and next 4 ingredients on a piece of cheesecloth; tie ends of cheesecloth securely. Add this bouquet garni to bean mixture. Cover, reduce heat, and simmer 1 hour.

Add 1 cup water and next 3 ingredients; cover and simmer 15 minutes. Add potato; cover mixture, and simmer 30 minutes or until vegetables are tender.

Remove ham hock from soup; let cool slightly. Chop meat, and add to soup. Discard ham bone and cheesecloth bag. Add hot sauce, salt, and pepper to soup. Stir well. **Yield: 3½ quarts.**

Bean 'n' Ham Soup Technique

A bouquet garni is a combination of herbs used to flavor soups; the herbs are tied in a cheesecloth bag for easy removal before serving.

Spicy Three-Bean Soup

2 skinned chicken breast halves
3 cups water
1 (28-ounce) can whole tomatoes, undrained and chopped
1 (10-ounce) package frozen cut green beans
1 (10-ounce) package frozen baby lima beans
1 bay leaf
2 teaspoons Creole seasoning
1 teaspoon chili powder
1 teaspoon paprika
¼ teaspoon garlic powder
¼ teaspoon onion powder
¼ teaspoon red pepper
Dash of hot sauce
Dash of soy sauce
Dash of Worcestershire sauce
1 (15-ounce) can black beans, drained

Combine all ingredients, except black beans, in a Dutch oven. Bring to a boil over medium heat. Cover, reduce heat, and simmer 1 hour.

Remove chicken from soup; cool, bone, and cut into bite-size pieces. Return chicken to Dutch oven; add black beans, and heat thoroughly. **Yield 2½ quarts.**

Navy Bean Soup

Navy Bean Soup

1 cup dried navy beans
5 cups water
½ cup chopped celery
½ cup chopped onion
½ cup chopped carrot
1 tablespoon chopped fresh parsley
1 chicken-flavored bouillon cube
½ cup diced cooked ham
1 bay leaf

Sort and wash beans; place in a large Dutch oven. Cover with water 2 inches above beans; let soak 8 hours.

Drain beans, and return to Dutch oven. Add 5 cups water and next 5 ingredients. Bring to a boil; cover, reduce heat, and simmer 45 minutes.

Add ham and bay leaf; cover and simmer 30 additional minutes. Remove bay leaf before serving. **Yield: 1½ quarts.**

Bean and Barley Soup

2 pounds dried Great Northern beans
2 quarts water
1 cup fine barley
1 ham hock
2 cups coarsely chopped ham
1 pound ground beef, cooked and drained
1 large onion, chopped
8 cloves garlic, chopped
6 carrots, sliced
4 (10½-ounce) cans beef consommé, undiluted
1 to 1½ teaspoons salt
1 teaspoon pepper
¼ cup Worcestershire sauce
½ teaspoon hot sauce
2 fresh jalapeño peppers, split and seeded

Sort and wash beans; place in a large Dutch oven. Cover with water 2 inches above beans; let soak 8 hours.

Drain beans, and return to Dutch oven. Add 2 quarts water; bring to a boil. Add barley and remaining ingredients; cover, reduce heat, and simmer 2½ hours, stirring occasionally. **Yield: 5½ quarts.**

Note: Add additional water for a thinner consistency, if desired.

Lentil Soup

1 pound dried lentils
1 pound smoked sausage, thinly sliced
1 stalk celery, chopped
4 cloves garlic, minced
½ to 1 teaspoon salt
½ teaspoon black peppercorns
½ teaspoon ground cumin

Sort and wash lentils; place in a Dutch oven. Cover with water 2 inches above lentils; bring to a boil. Cover, reduce heat, and simmer 40 minutes or until tender.

Brown sausage in a heavy skillet; drain. Add sausage, celery, and remaining ingredients to lentils; simmer 5 minutes. Remove peppercorns before serving. **Yield: 2½ quarts.**

Beefy Lentil Soup

1 cup dried lentils
½ pound round steak, cut into 1-inch cubes
3 medium carrots, sliced
1 large onion, chopped
1 small hot pepper, chopped
1 teaspoon salt
1 teaspoon freshly ground pepper
2 tablespoons olive oil
2 bay leaves
Dash of dried basil
6½ cups water
1 (14½-ounce) can stewed tomatoes, undrained
1 (6-ounce) can tomato juice

Sort and wash dried lentils; place in a Dutch oven. Cover with water 2 inches above lentils; let soak 8 hours.

Drain beans, and return to Dutch oven. Add round steak and next 9 ingredients to beans. Bring to a boil; cover, reduce heat, and simmer 1 hour, stirring occasionally.

Add tomato and tomato juice; cover and simmer 30 additional minutes. Remove bay leaves. **Yield: 2 quarts.**

Guadalajara Soup

(pictured on page 73)

1¼ cups dried pinto beans
3½ to 4 pounds country-style pork ribs
2 tablespoons vegetable oil
1 cup finely chopped onion
2 cloves garlic, minced
4 cups water
2 (14½-ounce) cans ready-to-serve beef broth
2 teaspoons chili powder
1 teaspoon dried oregano
1 teaspoon ground cumin
4 cups thinly sliced carrot
1 (7-ounce) jar baby corn on the cob, drained
½ teaspoon salt
¼ teaspoon pepper
Condiments: sour cream, jalapeño salsa,
   chopped fresh cilantro (optional)

Sort and wash beans; place in a Dutch oven. Cover with water 2 inches above beans. Cover and bring to a boil; boil 2 minutes. Remove from heat; let stand, covered, 1 hour. Drain beans, and set aside.

Brown short ribs in oil in Dutch oven over medium heat. Remove short ribs, reserving drippings in Dutch oven. Cook onion and garlic in drippings over medium-high heat, stirring constantly, until onion is tender.

Add beans, short ribs, 4 cups water, and next 4 ingredients to Dutch oven. Bring to a boil; cover, reduce heat, and simmer 1½ hours or until short ribs are tender, stirring occasionally.

Remove short ribs; let cool slightly. Remove meat from bones; discard fat and bones. Chop meat. Skim fat from broth mixture.

Add chopped meat, carrot, corn, salt, and pepper to Dutch oven. Bring to a boil; cover, reduce heat, and simmer 30 minutes or until carrot is tender. Serve soup with condiments, if desired. **Yield: about 3 quarts.**

Taco Soup

1½ pounds lean ground beef
1 large onion, chopped
2 large cloves garlic, minced
1 (1.25-ounce) package taco seasoning mix
1 (28-ounce) can whole tomatoes, undrained
   and chopped
2 (16-ounce) cans red kidney beans, drained
1 (15-ounce) can tomato sauce
1 (10½-ounce) can condensed beef broth,
   undiluted
2 (4.5-ounce) cans chopped green chiles,
   drained
3 tablespoons chopped jalapeño pepper
1½ cups water
1 teaspoon ground cumin
1 teaspoon chili powder
Condiments: finely shredded iceberg lettuce,
   chopped tomato, corn chips, shredded
   Cheddar cheese

Brown ground beef, onion, and garlic in a Dutch oven, stirring until beef crumbles. Drain well, and return to Dutch oven. Add taco seasoning mix; stir well.

Add tomato and next 8 ingredients. Bring to a boil; cover, reduce heat, and simmer 30 minutes.

Ladle soup into bowls; serve with condiments. **Yield: 3¾ quarts.**

Taco Soup

Sausage, Bacon, and Bean Soup

Sausage, Bacon, and Bean Soup

¾ pound smoked sausage, cut into ¾-inch-
    thick slices
4 slices thick-sliced peppered bacon, cut into
    1-inch pieces
2 medium onions, chopped
1 large green pepper, seeded and chopped
2 cloves garlic, minced
2 (15-ounce) cans kidney beans, drained
1 (28-ounce) can tomatoes, undrained and
    chopped
1 quart water
1 (8-ounce) can tomato sauce
1 bay leaf
½ teaspoon seasoned salt
½ teaspoon dried thyme
½ teaspoon pepper
2 cups peeled, coarsely chopped potato
¼ cup chopped fresh parsley

Cook sausage in a large skillet until browned;
remove from heat, and set aside.

Cook bacon in a Dutch oven until crisp. Remove bacon, and set aside, reserving 1 tablespoon drippings in Dutch oven. Add onion, green
pepper, and garlic to Dutch oven; cook 2 minutes,
stirring constantly.

Add kidney beans and next 7 ingredients.
Bring to a boil; cover, reduce heat, and simmer
30 minutes. Add chopped potato; cover and simmer 30 additional minutes.

Add reserved sausage; cover and simmer 30 to
40 minutes or until vegetables are tender. Remove bay leaf. Add bacon, and sprinkle with
parsley before serving. **Yield: 3½ quarts.**

Mexican Pork and Bean Soup

1 pound boneless pork loin chops, cut into
    cubes
1 tablespoon butter or margarine, melted
1 tablespoon olive oil
2 medium onions, chopped
3 cloves garlic, minced
3 (14½-ounce) cans ready-to-serve chicken
    broth
3 (16-ounce) cans pinto beans, rinsed and
    drained
1¼ teaspoons dried oregano
¾ teaspoon cumin seeds
½ teaspoon pepper
Vegetable oil
12 (6-inch) corn tortillas, cut into 2- x ¼-inch
    strips
2 (3-ounce) packages cream cheese, cut into
    cubes
Condiments: shredded lettuce, chopped
    tomato, sliced green onions, chopped fresh
    cilantro

Cook pork in butter and olive oil in a Dutch
oven over medium-high heat until browned.
Remove pork with a slotted spoon, reserving
drippings in Dutch oven. Drain pork on paper
towels; set aside.

Cook onion and garlic in reserved drippings
over medium heat, stirring constantly, 3 to 5 minutes or until onion is tender.

Add pork, chicken broth, and next 4 ingredients. Bring to a boil; cover, reduce heat, and simmer 20 to 30 minutes.

Pour oil to depth of 1 inch into a heavy skillet.
Fry one-fourth of tortilla strips in hot oil over
medium heat until browned. Remove strips; drain
on paper towels. Repeat procedure with remaining tortilla strips.

Ladle soup into bowls; top with tortilla strips
and cream cheese cubes. Serve with condiments.
Yield: 2¾ quarts.

Italian Spinach Soup with Meatballs

3 quarts ready-to-serve chicken broth
2 stalks celery, cut into chunks
2 carrots, scraped and cut into chunks
1 large onion, quartered
½ teaspoon salt
1 pound lean ground beef
1½ slices bread, crumbled
1 large egg, lightly beaten
2 tablespoons grated Parmesan cheese
1½ tablespoons chopped fresh parsley
½ teaspoon salt
¼ teaspoon ground white pepper
1 (16-ounce) can crushed Italian-style
  tomatoes, undrained
1 (10-ounce) package frozen chopped spinach,
  thawed and drained
2 tablespoons grated Parmesan cheese
3 tablespoons olive oil
2 tablespoons lemon juice
2 teaspoons dried basil
4 cloves garlic, crushed

Combine first 5 ingredients in a large Dutch oven. Bring to a boil; reduce heat, and simmer, uncovered, 30 minutes. Remove vegetables, and discard. Set broth aside.

Combine ground beef and next 6 ingredients; shape into 1-inch meatballs, and cook in a large nonstick skillet over medium heat until browned. Drain on paper towels.

Bring broth to a boil; add meatballs. Reduce heat, and simmer 10 minutes. Stir in tomatoes and remaining ingredients; simmer 10 to 15 minutes. **Yield: 3 quarts.**

Steak Soup

2 tablespoons vegetable oil
2 pounds lean boneless round steak, cut into
  1-inch cubes
Salt and freshly ground pepper
1 medium onion, chopped
2 cloves garlic, minced
5 cups water
½ cup Worcestershire sauce
1 teaspoon cracked pepper
½ teaspoon paprika
2½ cups medium egg noodles, uncooked
  (about 6 ounces)
2 cups sliced fresh mushrooms
2 cups (8 ounces) shredded Cheddar cheese

Heat oil in a Dutch oven over medium-high heat. Add meat, and sprinkle generously with salt and pepper. Brown meat on all sides, stirring occasionally.

Add onion and garlic; cook 2 minutes, stirring occasionally. Add water and next 3 ingredients. Bring to a boil; cover, reduce heat, and simmer 1 hour and 15 minutes.

Stir in egg noodles and mushrooms. Bring mixture to a boil; cover, reduce heat, and simmer 30 minutes or until meat is tender and noodles are cooked.

Ladle soup into individual serving bowls; top with shredded cheese. **Yield: about 1¾ quarts.**

Steak Soup

Chunky Vegetable-Beef Soup

Chunky Vegetable-Beef Soup

3 pounds beef short ribs
2½ quarts water
3 stalks celery with leaves, thinly sliced
1 large onion, quartered
4 fresh parsley sprigs
1 tablespoon salt
12 black peppercorns
1 bay leaf
2 (28-ounce) cans whole tomatoes, undrained
1 cup shredded cabbage
1 cup thinly sliced leeks
1 medium potato, peeled and chopped
1 medium sweet potato, peeled and chopped
1 turnip, peeled and chopped
¾ cup scraped and thinly sliced carrot
¼ cup chopped fresh parsley
½ (10-ounce) package frozen baby lima beans
½ (10-ounce) package frozen whole kernel corn
½ cup ditalini (small tubular pasta), uncooked
1 medium zucchini, halved lengthwise and thinly sliced
½ (9-ounce) package frozen cut green beans
½ (10-ounce) package frozen English peas
1 tablespoon sugar
1 teaspoon salt
½ teaspoon pepper
½ teaspoon dried basil
½ teaspoon dried oregano

Combine first 8 ingredients in a large Dutch oven. Bring to a boil; cover, reduce heat, and simmer 2 hours. Remove from heat.

Remove short ribs, and let cool. Remove meat from bones; discard fat and bones. Cut meat into ½-inch pieces, and set aside.

Pour soup stock through a large wire-mesh strainer into a large bowl, discarding solids; skim off fat. Return stock to Dutch oven; add meat, tomatoes and next 7 ingredients. Bring to a boil; cover, reduce heat, and simmer 15 minutes.

Stir in lima beans, corn, and pasta; cover and simmer 5 minutes. Add zucchini and remaining ingredients; cover and simmer 10 minutes or until vegetables and pasta are tender. **Yield: 6 quarts.**

Ground Beef Soup

1 pound ground beef
1 cup chopped onion
2 cloves garlic, crushed
1 (30-ounce) jar chunky garden-style spaghetti sauce with mushrooms and peppers
1 (10½-ounce) can condensed beef broth, undiluted
2 cups water
1 cup sliced celery
1 teaspoon sugar
1 teaspoon salt
½ teaspoon freshly ground pepper
1 (10-ounce) can diced tomatoes and green chiles
1 (16-ounce) package frozen mixed vegetables

Cook first 3 ingredients in a large Dutch oven over medium heat until meat is browned, stirring to crumble. Drain and return meat to Dutch oven.

Add spaghetti sauce and next 6 ingredients. Bring to a boil; cover, reduce heat, and simmer 20 minutes, stirring occasionally.

Stir in tomatoes and vegetables; return to a boil. Cover and simmer 10 to 12 minutes or until vegetables are tender. **Yield: 3 quarts.**

Chicken Noodle Soup

1 (3½- to 4-pound) broiler-fryer, halved
2 stalks celery, halved
1 large onion, quartered
1 carrot, scraped and halved
1 turnip, peeled and halved
2 cloves garlic, crushed
1¼ teaspoons salt
¾ teaspoon pepper
¼ teaspoon dried tarragon
4 cups water
3 cups ready-to-serve chicken broth
4 ounces medium egg noodles, uncooked
1 large onion, chopped
2 stalks celery, sliced
2 carrots, scraped and sliced
½ teaspoon salt
½ teaspoon pepper
¼ teaspoon tarragon

Combine first 11 ingredients in a large Dutch oven, and bring mixture to a boil over high heat. Reduce heat, and cook 45 minutes or until chicken is tender.

Remove chicken from broth, reserving broth; set chicken aside to cool slightly.

Pour broth through a wire-mesh strainer into a large bowl; discard vegetables. Remove and discard fat from broth; return broth to Dutch oven.

Cook noodles according to package directions, omitting salt and fat; drain and set aside.

Skin and bone cooked chicken; chop chicken, and set aside.

Add chopped onion, sliced celery, and sliced carrot to chicken broth; bring to a boil over high heat. Reduce heat; simmer 15 minutes.

Stir in chopped chicken and noodles; add ½ teaspoon salt and remaining ingredients. Cook until thoroughly heated. **Yield: 2½ quarts.**

Garden Chicken Noodle Soup

2 (8-ounce) chicken breast halves, skinned
1½ quarts water
1 cup frozen green peas
1 medium-size yellow squash, thinly sliced
½ cup thinly sliced carrot
½ cup chopped celery
½ cup chopped onion
1 tablespoon chicken-flavored bouillon
   granules
1 teaspoon salt
¼ teaspoon pepper
2 cups uncooked medium egg noodles

Arrange chicken in a deep 3-quart baking dish; add water. Stir in green peas and next 7 ingredients.

Cover with heavy-duty plastic wrap; fold back a small edge of wrap to allow steam to escape. Microwave at HIGH 20 to 25 minutes or until boiling.

Stir in noodles. Reduce to MEDIUM (50% power); cover and microwave 20 to 30 minutes or until noodles and chicken are tender, stirring every 10 minutes.

Remove chicken from soup; let cool. Skim excess fat from soup. Bone chicken, and cut meat into bite-size pieces; return chicken to soup.

Cover and microwave at HIGH 5 to 6 minutes or until soup is thoroughly heated. Serve immediately. **Yield: 2 quarts.**

Garden Chicken Noodle Soup

Chicken-Rice Soup

broth. Let chicken cool. Bone chicken; coarsely chop meat, and set aside.

Remove and discard fat from broth. Bring broth to a boil. Add rice and next 7 ingredients; cover and cook 20 minutes or until rice and vegetables are tender, stirring occasionally.

Stir in chicken, and cook until thoroughly heated. **Yield: 2¼ quarts.**

Mexican Chicken Soup

1 (3- to 3½-pound) broiler-fryer
1½ quarts water
3 stalks celery
1 medium onion, sliced
1 teaspoon salt
⅛ teaspoon pepper
1 tablespoon plus 1 teaspoon chicken-flavored bouillon granules
3 medium carrots, thinly sliced
1 medium onion, chopped
1 (16-ounce) can tomatoes, undrained and chopped
1 small zucchini, thinly sliced
1 cup frozen English peas

Combine first 6 ingredients in a Dutch oven; bring to a boil. Cover, reduce heat, and simmer 1 hour or until chicken is tender. Remove chicken from broth; let cool. Bone chicken; cut into bite-size pieces.

Pour broth through a wire-mesh strainer into a large bowl, discarding vegetables. Remove and discard fat from broth; return broth to Dutch oven. Add bouillon granules and next 3 ingredients; cover and simmer 30 minutes.

Add chicken, zucchini, and peas; cover and simmer 10 to 15 additional minutes or until vegetables are tender. **Yield: 1½ quarts.**

Chicken-Rice Soup

1 (2½- to 3-pound) broiler-fryer, cut in half and skinned
2 quarts water
1 cup long-grain rice, uncooked
2 carrots, scraped and sliced
1 stalk celery, chopped
1 medium onion, chopped
2 cloves garlic, crushed
1 tablespoon chicken-flavored bouillon granules
2 teaspoons salt
¼ teaspoon pepper

Combine chicken and water in a Dutch oven; bring to a boil. Cover, reduce heat, and simmer 40 minutes or until chicken is tender.

Remove chicken from Dutch oven, and reserve

Turkey-Rice Soup

¾ pound turkey tenderloin, cut into bite-size
     pieces
1½ quarts water
2 stalks celery, sliced
1 medium onion, chopped
2 chicken-flavored bouillon cubes
1 teaspoon salt
¼ teaspoon poultry seasoning
1 bay leaf
½ cup long-grain rice, uncooked
2 carrots, scraped and sliced

Combine first 8 ingredients in a Dutch oven.
Bring to a boil; cover, reduce heat, and simmer
40 minutes.

Add rice and carrot; cover and simmer 20
additional minutes or until rice is tender. Remove
bay leaf. **Yield: 1½ quarts.**

Turkey-Noodle Soup

1 turkey carcass
4 quarts water
½ cup finely chopped onion
½ cup finely chopped celery
1 teaspoon salt
¼ teaspoon pepper
4 ounces medium egg noodles, uncooked

Place turkey carcass and water in a large
Dutch oven; bring to a boil. Cover, reduce heat,
and simmer 1 hour.

Remove carcass from broth, and pick meat
from bones; set meat aside. Measure 8 cups
broth, and return it to Dutch oven. (Chill remaining broth for other uses.)

Add onion and next 3 ingredients to broth in
Dutch oven. Bring to a boil; cover, reduce heat,
and simmer 1 hour.

Stir in turkey and noodles; simmer, uncovered, 8 minutes or until noodles are tender.
Yield: 2 quarts.

Turkey-Vegetable Soup

1 turkey carcass
4 quarts water
1 small onion, chopped
2 tablespoons butter or margarine, melted
2 medium potatoes, peeled and diced
2 carrots, scraped and diced
½ cup chopped celery
1 teaspoon salt
⅛ teaspoon pepper
2 tablespoons all-purpose flour
2½ cups milk, divided

Place turkey carcass and water in a large
Dutch oven; bring to a boil. Cover, reduce heat,
and simmer 1 hour.

Remove carcass from broth, and pick meat
from bones; set meat aside. Measure and set aside
2 cups turkey broth. (Chill remaining broth for
other uses.)

Cook onion in butter in Dutch oven over
medium heat, stirring constantly, until tender.
Add 2 cups broth, turkey, potato, and next 4
ingredients. Bring mixture to a boil; cover, reduce
heat, and simmer 10 minutes or until vegetables
are tender.

Combine flour and ½ cup milk, stirring until
smooth; add remaining milk, and stir into turkey
mixture. Cook over medium heat until soup is
slightly thickened, stirring occasionally. **Yield:
1¾ quarts.**

Louisiana Oyster and Artichoke Soup

2 (12-ounce) containers fresh Standard oysters, undrained
½ cup finely chopped shallots
1 bay leaf
⅛ to ¼ teaspoon ground red pepper
Pinch of dried thyme
3 tablespoons butter or margarine, melted
2 tablespoons all-purpose flour
1 (14½-ounce) can ready-to-serve chicken broth
1 (14-ounce) can artichoke hearts, drained and cut into eighths
1 tablespoon chopped fresh parsley
½ teaspoon salt
⅛ to ¼ teaspoon hot sauce
½ cup whipping cream

Drain oysters, reserving 1 cup liquid. Cut each oyster into fourths; set oysters and liquid aside.

Cook shallots and next 3 ingredients in butter in a Dutch oven over medium heat, stirring constantly, until shallots are tender.

Add flour, stirring until smooth. Cook, stirring constantly, 1 minute. Gradually add chicken broth and oyster liquid; simmer, stirring occasionally, 15 minutes. Remove bay leaf.

Add oysters, artichoke hearts, and next 3 ingredients; simmer mixture 10 minutes. Stir in whipping cream; cook until thoroughly heated. **Yield: 1½ quarts.**

Microwave Directions:

Drain oysters, reserving 1 cup liquid. Cut each oyster into fourths, and set oysters and reserved liquid aside.

Place chopped shallots, bay leaf, ground red pepper, and thyme in a 3-quart baking dish. Add melted butter, and microwave at HIGH 3 minutes, stirring after 2 minutes.

Add flour, stirring until smooth. Gradually add broth and reserved oyster liquid, stirring well.

Microwave at HIGH 9 to 10 minutes, stirring after 5 minutes. Remove bay leaf.

Add oysters, artichoke hearts, and next 3 ingredients; microwave at HIGH 5 to 8 minutes, stirring mixture after 4 minutes. Stir in whipping cream. Serve immediately.

Artichoke-Seafood Soup

2 (12-ounce) containers fresh Standard oysters, undrained
¼ cup butter or margarine
¼ cup all-purpose flour
2 cups milk
1½ cups half-and-half
1¼ cups freshly grated Parmesan cheese, divided
1 (14-ounce) can artichoke hearts, drained and coarsely chopped
1 (12-ounce) container fresh lump crabmeat
2 tablespoons chopped fresh chives
¼ teaspoon pepper
2 tablespoons Sauterne
Additional chopped fresh chives

Drain oysters, reserving ½ cup liquid; set oysters aside.

Melt butter in a 3-quart saucepan over low heat; add flour, stirring until smooth. Cook, stirring constantly, until golden. Gradually stir in milk and half-and-half.

Add reserved oyster liquid and ¾ cup Parmesan cheese. Cook over medium heat, stirring constantly, until thickened and bubbly.

Add oysters, chopped artichokes, and next 3 ingredients; simmer mixture 4 to 5 minutes or until edges of oysters curl and soup is thoroughly heated. Stir in wine.

Ladle soup into individual serving bowls. Sprinkle with remaining ½ cup Parmesan cheese and chopped fresh chives. **Yield: about 2 quarts.**

Artichoke-Seafood Soup

Southern Bouillabaisse

1 large onion, coarsely chopped
2 cloves garlic, minced
¼ cup butter or margarine, melted
2 tablespoons all-purpose flour
2 cups water
1 cup coarsely chopped fresh tomato
1 (8-ounce) can tomato sauce
½ cup dry sherry
1 bay leaf
1 teaspoon salt
¼ teaspoon ground red pepper
¼ teaspoon dried thyme
⅛ teaspoon ground allspice
Pinch of ground saffron
1 pound unpeeled medium-size fresh shrimp
2 pounds red snapper, skinned and cut into
    large pieces
1 (12-ounce) container fresh Standard oysters,
    undrained
Toasted French bread

Cook onion and garlic in butter in a large Dutch oven over medium heat, stirring constantly, until tender. Add flour, stirring until smooth. Cook 1 minute, stirring constantly. Gradually stir in water.

Add tomato and next 8 ingredients. Bring mixture to a boil; reduce heat, and simmer, uncovered, 30 minutes.

Peel shrimp, and devein, if desired. Add shrimp, fish, and oysters; simmer 5 minutes or until shrimp turn pink and fish flakes easily when tested with a fork. Remove bay leaf. Serve each portion over a slice of toasted French bread. **Yield: 2½ quarts.**

Gulf Coast Cioppino

20 fresh mussels
20 fresh clams
¼ cup butter or margarine
1 tablespoon olive oil
2 cups chopped celery
2 cups chopped green pepper
1 cup chopped green onions
2 cloves garlic, crushed
1 (16-ounce) can crushed tomatoes, undrained
1 (15-ounce) can tomato sauce
1 to 1½ tablespoons dried Italian seasoning
1 to 1½ teaspoons ground red pepper
1½ teaspoons paprika
1 teaspoon sugar
1 teaspoon salt
½ teaspoon ground black pepper
2 (14½-ounce) cans ready-to-serve chicken
    broth
1 pound grouper, amberjack, or sea bass
    fillets, cut into bite-size pieces

Scrub mussels with a brush, removing beards. Wash clams. Discard any opened mussels and clams. Set aside.

Melt butter in a large Dutch oven over medium heat. Add olive oil and next 4 ingredients; cook, stirring constantly, 5 minutes or until vegetables are tender.

Stir in tomatoes and next 7 ingredients; cook mixture 2 to 3 minutes, stirring occasionally. Stir in chicken broth.

Bring tomato mixture to a boil; reduce heat, and simmer 45 minutes, stirring occasionally.

Stir in mussels, clams, and fish; cook 3 to 4 minutes, stirring occasionally. (Mussels and clams should open during cooking. Discard any unopened shells.) Serve immediately. **Yield: about 3 quarts.**

Stews & Burgoos

Seasoned with herbs and spices and simmered to perfection, heart-warming stews and burgoos are nutritious as well as simple to prepare. And most of them require only one pot for cooking.

Irish Stew, White Wine Stew with Dumplings, Mexican Stew Olé

Hearty Lamb Stew, Beef or Lamb Stew with Popovers, Venison Sausage Stew

Old-Fashioned Burgoo, Kentucky Burgoo, Virginia Brunswick Stew, Lamb Stew

Pancho Villa Stew, Holiday Oyster Stew, Bama Brunswick Stew

Burgundy Beef Stew (page 100)

Burgundy Beef Stew

(pictured on page 99)

1 cup Burgundy or other dry red wine
1 (8-ounce) can tomato sauce
2 tablespoons red wine vinegar
2 cloves garlic, crushed
2 bay leaves
½ teaspoon pepper
¼ teaspoon ground allspice
2½ pounds beef stew meat, cut into 1-inch
     cubes
¼ cup olive oil
2 (10½-ounce) cans condensed beef broth,
     undiluted
1 (9-ounce) package frozen green beans
½ pound fresh mushrooms, halved
1 medium onion, coarsely chopped
3 carrots, scraped and diagonally sliced
2 tablespoons all-purpose flour
2 tablespoons water

Combine first 7 ingredients in a large shallow dish; stir well. Add stew meat; cover and marinate in refrigerator 8 hours.

Drain meat, reserving marinade. Remove bay leaves; set marinade aside.

Heat olive oil in a Dutch oven over medium heat; add meat, and cook until browned on all sides. Drain and return meat to Dutch oven.

Add reserved marinade and beef broth to Dutch oven. Bring to a boil; cover, reduce heat, and simmer 1½ hours. Add green beans and next 3 ingredients, stirring well; cover and cook 30 minutes or until vegetables are tender.

Combine flour and water, stirring until smooth. Stir into stew, and cook until slightly thickened. **Yield: 2¼ quarts.**

Irish Stew

1 cup dry red wine
1 clove garlic, minced
2 bay leaves
1 teaspoon salt
½ teaspoon freshly ground pepper
¼ teaspoon dried thyme
3 pounds beef stew meat, cut into 1-inch
     cubes
¼ cup olive oil
2 (10½-ounce) cans condensed beef broth,
     undiluted
6 carrots, scraped and cut into 2-inch slices
12 small boiling onions
6 medium potatoes, peeled and halved

Combine first 6 ingredients in a large shallow dish; stir well. Add stew meat; cover and marinate in refrigerator 8 hours.

Drain meat, reserving marinade. Remove bay leaves; set marinade aside.

Heat oil in a Dutch oven over medium heat; brown beef in oil. Add beef broth and reserved marinade; bring to a boil. Cover, reduce heat, and simmer 1½ hours.

Add carrot, onions, and potato; cover and cook 30 minutes. **Yield: 2½ quarts.**

Meats for Stew

Using stew meat or less tender cuts of beef, lamb, or pork is economical when making stew. The long simmering time of most of these dishes will help tenderize the meat.

Irish Stew

White Wine Stew with Dumplings

White Wine Stew with Dumplings

¼ cup plus 1 tablespoon flour
1 teaspoon salt
½ teaspoon pepper
1¼ pounds boneless beef chuck roast, cut into 1-inch cubes
3 tablespoons butter or margarine
2 cups water
1½ cups dry white wine
1 cup chopped onion
2 cloves garlic, minced
2 teaspoons beef-flavored bouillon granules

1 bay leaf
⅛ teaspoon dried thyme
2 medium carrots, scraped and sliced
1 large potato, peeled and cubed
1 cup frozen green peas
¼ cup sliced celery
1 cup biscuit mix
1 large egg, beaten
3 tablespoons milk
1 tablespoon plus 1 teaspoon minced fresh parsley

Combine first 3 ingredients; dredge beef in flour mixture. Place a 10-inch browning skillet in microwave oven; preheat, uncovered, at HIGH 6 minutes.

Add butter to hot skillet, tilting to coat surface. Add beef to skillet, stirring well. Microwave, uncovered, at HIGH 6 minutes or until beef is browned, stirring after 3 minutes.

Combine beef, water, and next 6 ingredients in a deep 3-quart baking dish. Cover with heavy-duty plastic wrap; fold back a small edge of wrap to allow steam to escape. Microwave at HIGH 5 minutes.

Stir in carrot and next 3 ingredients. Reduce to MEDIUM (50% power); cover and microwave 75 to 80 minutes or until vegetables and beef are tender, stirring every 20 minutes. Remove bay leaf.

Combine biscuit mix and next 3 ingredients, stirring well. Drop mixture by heaping tablespoonfuls on top of stew. Increase to HIGH; cover and microwave 3½ to 4 minutes or until dumplings are set, but still moist. Let stand, covered, 5 minutes. **Yield: 2 quarts.**

Red Chili Stew

1½ pounds lean beef chuck roast, cut into
     1-inch cubes
2 cups water
3 tablespoons ground red chile or chili powder
1 teaspoon salt
1 teaspoon ground oregano
1 clove garlic, crushed
3 large tomatoes, chopped

Combine beef and water in a Dutch oven; bring to a boil over medium-high heat. Cover, reduce heat, and simmer 45 minutes or until tender, stirring occasionally.

Stir in ground chile and remaining ingredients; cook 30 additional minutes. **Yield: 1 quart.**

Mexican Stew Olé

1½ pounds beef stew meat, cut into 1-inch
     cubes
¼ cup all-purpose flour
¼ cup vegetable oil
1 large onion, chopped
1 clove garlic, minced
2 (4.5-ounce) cans chopped green chiles,
     drained
½ teaspoon salt
1 teaspoon coarsely ground pepper
2 tablespoons red wine vinegar
1 cup dry red wine
1 (15-ounce) can tomato sauce
1 cup water

Dredge stew meat in flour; cook in hot oil in a Dutch oven over medium heat until meat is browned.

Add onion and remaining ingredients; stir well. Cover, reduce heat, and simmer 1 hour, stirring occasionally. **Yield: 1½ quarts.**

Flavor Boosters

• Madeira or sherry enhances the flavor of seafood or chicken soups and stews while red wine or beer adds flavor to beef stews.

• Leftover pan juices or cooking liquids from meats and vegetables enrich soups and stews.

• Some fresh herbs lose flavor when cooked a long time. Taste the stew before serving, and add additional herbs, if necessary.

Beef Stew with Popovers

Beef or Lamb Stew with Popovers

1 medium onion, chopped
1 clove garlic, crushed
1 tablespoon olive oil
¼ cup all-purpose flour
2 (14½-ounce) cans ready-to-serve chicken
    broth
½ cup dry white wine
2 tablespoons lemon juice
1 teaspoon salt
¼ teaspoon dried marjoram
¼ teaspoon dried rosemary
⅛ teaspoon pepper
1 bay leaf
12 pearl onions
6 small new potatoes, peeled and thinly sliced
3 carrots, scraped and cut into 1-inch pieces
3 cups cubed cooked beef or lamb
Popovers
Garnish: fresh rosemary sprigs

Cook onion and garlic in olive oil in a Dutch oven over medium heat, stirring constantly, until tender. Sprinkle with flour, stirring well.

Stir in chicken broth and next 7 ingredients. Bring to a boil; cover, reduce heat, and simmer 30 minutes.

Add pearl onions, potato, and carrot; cover and simmer 20 to 30 minutes or until vegetables are tender. Remove bay leaf.

Stir in beef or lamb, and cook until thoroughly heated. Serve with Popovers. Garnish, if desired. **Yield: 1¾ quarts.**

Popovers

1 cup all-purpose flour
¼ teaspoon salt
1 cup milk
2 large eggs, lightly beaten

Combine all ingredients; beat at low speed of an electric mixer just until smooth.

Heat a well-greased 3½-inch muffin pan or popover pan in a 450° oven 3 minutes or until a drop of water sizzles when dropped in pan. Remove pan from oven; fill half full with batter.

Bake at 450° for 15 minutes. Reduce heat to 350°, and bake 20 to 25 additional minutes. Serve immediately. **Yield: 6 popovers.**

Lamb Stew

Juice of 2 lemons
3 pounds boneless lamb shoulder, cubed
6 cups cold water
4 medium potatoes, peeled and quartered
3 medium onions, sliced
3 to 4 cloves garlic, chopped
2 chicken-flavored bouillon cubes
½ teaspoon salt
½ teaspoon freshly ground pepper
6 cups water
8 small boiling onions, sliced
8 small new potatoes, peeled and quartered
8 baby carrots, scraped and cut in half
1½ teaspoons minced fresh thyme or
    ½ teaspoon dried thyme

Drizzle lemon juice over lamb, and let stand 10 minutes. Place lamb in a large Dutch oven; add 6 cups cold water. Bring to a boil; reduce heat, and simmer 5 minutes. Drain and discard liquid. Rinse lamb and Dutch oven with cold water.

Return lamb to Dutch oven; add 4 potatoes and next 6 ingredients. Bring to a boil; reduce heat, and simmer, uncovered, 1½ hours.

Remove potatoes and onions; place in container of a food processor or blender. Add ¼ cup cooking liquid, and process until smooth; stir into lamb mixture.

Add 8 onions and remaining ingredients; cover and simmer 30 minutes. **Yield: 3½ quarts.**

Hearty Lamb Stew

Hearty Lamb Stew

2 pounds boneless lamb or top round beef
    steak, cut into 1½-inch cubes
¼ cup all-purpose flour
1 clove garlic, crushed
2 tablespoons vegetable oil
3 cups water
1 (8-ounce) can tomato sauce
1 tablespoon beef-flavored bouillon granules
1 teaspoon salt
¼ teaspoon pepper
1 teaspoon dried thyme
1 teaspoon dried parsley flakes
1 bay leaf
4 medium potatoes, peeled and cubed
12 carrots, scraped and sliced
1 (10-ounce) package frozen English peas

Dredge meat in flour. Brown meat and garlic in oil in a large Dutch oven over medium heat, stirring constantly.

Add 3 cups water and remaining ingredients.

Bring to a boil; cover, reduce heat, and simmer 1 hour or until meat is tender. Remove bay leaf. **Yield: 2 quarts.**

Note: Stew may be frozen in an airtight container up to 3 months.

Pancho Villa Stew

½ pound chorizo, casings removed
2 pounds boneless pork loin, cut into 1-inch
   cubes
¼ cup all-purpose flour
2 tablespoons vegetable oil
3 (14½-ounce) cans ready-to-serve chicken
   broth
1 (14½-ounce) can whole tomatoes, drained
   and chopped
3 (4.5-ounce) cans chopped green chiles,
   undrained
1 large purple onion, sliced into rings
3 cloves garlic, crushed
2 teaspoons ground cumin
2 teaspoons cocoa
1 teaspoon dried oregano
¼ teaspoon salt
1 (2-inch) stick cinnamon
2 (15-ounce) cans black beans, rinsed and
   drained
1 (15½-ounce) can white hominy, rinsed and
   drained
1 (10-ounce) package frozen whole kernel
   corn
½ cup beer or tequila
Flour tortillas
Butter or margarine

Brown chorizo in a Dutch oven, stirring until it crumbles; drain well, and set aside.

Dredge pork in flour. Brown pork in oil in Dutch oven over medium heat. Stir in chorizo, chicken broth, and next 9 ingredients. Bring to a boil; reduce heat, and simmer 1 hour.

Stir in black beans and next 3 ingredients; cover and simmer 30 minutes. Remove cinnamon stick. Set stew aside, and keep warm.

Wrap tortillas tightly in aluminum foil; bake at 350° for 15 minutes or until thoroughly heated. Spread warm tortillas with butter, and serve with stew. **Yield: 1 gallon.**

Venison Sausage Stew

2 pounds venison summer sausage, cut into
   ¼-inch slices
1 large onion, chopped
1 green pepper, seeded and chopped
2 tablespoons butter or margarine, melted
2 (14½-ounce) cans stewed tomatoes,
   undrained
2 cups diced carrot
2 cups cubed unpeeled potato
1 teaspoon dried thyme
1 teaspoon dried oregano
1 bay leaf
1 (17-ounce) can whole kernel corn, drained
1 tablespoon all-purpose flour
¼ cup water

Cook first 3 ingredients in butter in a large Dutch oven until sausage is browned. Drain and return to Dutch oven.

Add tomatoes and next 5 ingredients. Bring to a boil; cover, reduce heat, and simmer 30 minutes, stirring occasionally. Add corn; cook until thoroughly heated.

Combine flour and water, stirring until smooth; stir into sausage mixture. Cook, stirring constantly, until thickened. Remove bay leaf.
Yield: 2½ quarts.

Note: You may substitute other types of summer sausage for venison sausage.

What's Chorizo?

Chorizo is a coarsely ground pork sausage that's seasoned with lots of garlic and chili powder. It provides a spicy flavor to many Mexican and Spanish recipes.

Venison Stew

2 pounds boneless venison, cubed
½ cup all-purpose flour
¼ cup bacon drippings
4 carrots, cut into ½-inch slices
2 (10½-ounce) cans beef broth, undiluted
2 cups dry red wine
2 bay leaves
1 (10½-ounce) can French onion soup, undiluted
1 large onion, coarsely chopped
1 large green pepper, seeded and coarsely chopped
¼ teaspoon salt
¼ teaspoon pepper
Hot cooked rice or biscuits (optional)

Dredge venison in flour; brown in hot bacon drippings in a large Dutch oven.

Add carrot and next 8 ingredients; cover, reduce heat, and simmer 2 hours. Remove bay leaves. Serve over rice or biscuits, if desired. **Yield: 2½ quarts.**

Hunter's Stew

1½ pounds boneless venison, cubed
½ pound smoked sausage, cut into ½-inch slices
2 tablespoons vegetable oil
½ cup chopped onion
½ cup chopped celery
2 (28-ounce) cans tomatoes, chopped
1 (12-ounce) can beer
1 teaspoon salt
1 teaspoon sugar
½ teaspoon dried rosemary
½ teaspoon dried basil
½ teaspoon freshly ground pepper
2 carrots, diced
2 medium potatoes, cubed

Brown venison and sausage in oil in a large Dutch oven. Add onion and celery; cook, stirring constantly, until onion is tender.

Add tomato and next 6 ingredients; cover, reduce heat, and simmer 30 minutes. Add carrot; cook, uncovered, 30 minutes. Add potato, and cook 30 additional minutes or until tender. **Yield: about 2 quarts.**

Frogmore Stew

¼ cup Old Bay seasoning
4 pounds small red potatoes
2 pounds kielbasa or hot, smoked link sausage, cut into 1½-inch slices
6 ears fresh corn, halved
4 pounds unpeeled large fresh shrimp
Additional Old Bay seasoning
Commercial cocktail sauce

Fill large container of a propane cooker halfway with water; add ¼ cup Old Bay seasoning. Bring to a boil, following manufacturer's instructions.

Add potatoes; return to a boil, and cook 10 minutes. Add sausage and corn; return to a boil, and cook 10 minutes or until potatoes are tender.

Add shrimp; cook 3 to 5 minutes or until shrimp turn pink.

Remove potatoes, sausage, corn, and shrimp with a slotted spoon onto a serving platter or newspaper-lined table. Serve with additional Old Bay seasoning and cocktail sauce. **Yield: 12 servings.**

Note: Frogmore Stew, a hallmark of Lowcountry hospitality, is a casual way to entertain a crowd. It may be cooked indoors in a large Dutch oven on a cooktop over high heat, if desired.

Potato-Oyster Stew

1 (12-ounce) container fresh Standard oysters,
    undrained
1 medium-size red potato,
    peeled and cubed
3 cups water
½ teaspoon salt
1 medium onion, chopped
1 stalk celery, chopped
⅓ cup butter or margarine, melted
¼ cup all-purpose flour
2 cups half-and-half
¼ teaspoon garlic powder
¼ teaspoon pepper
2 teaspoons chopped fresh parsley
Garnish: chopped fresh parsley

Drain oysters, reserving liquid. Using kitchen shears, cut through oysters 6 to 8 times. Set aside.

Combine potato, water, and salt in a medium saucepan. Bring to a boil; cover, reduce heat, and simmer 15 minutes or until tender. Drain, reserving liquid.

Cook onion and celery in butter in a 3-quart saucepan until tender. Stir in flour, and cook 1 minute, stirring constantly.

Add reserved potato liquid and half-and-half gradually; cook over medium heat, stirring constantly, until mixture slightly thickens.

Stir in potato, oysters, reserved oyster liquid, garlic powder, and next 2 ingredients. Simmer 8 to 10 minutes or until edges of oysters curl. Garnish, if desired. **Yield: 1½ quarts.**

Potato-Oyster Stew

Black-Eyed Pea Stew

Holiday Oyster Stew

2 tablespoons butter or margarine
1½ tablespoons all-purpose flour
3 cups milk
1 cup half-and-half
1 (12-ounce) container fresh Standard oysters,
    undrained
2 tablespoons butter or margarine
1½ teaspoons salt
Dash of hot sauce

Melt 2 tablespoons butter in a heavy saucepan over low heat; add flour, stirring until smooth. Cook 1 minute, stirring constantly.

Add milk and half-and-half gradually; cook over medium heat, stirring constantly, until mixture is bubbly.

Add oysters with liquid and remaining ingredients. Reduce heat, and simmer, stirring constantly, 5 to 8 minutes or until edges of oysters curl. **Yield: about 1¼ quarts.**

Black-Eyed Pea Stew

1 (16-ounce) package dried black-eyed peas
1 meaty ham hock
1 (10½-ounce) can beef consommé, undiluted
2 bay leaves
6 cups water, divided
3 stalks celery, chopped
1 large onion, chopped
1 large green pepper, seeded and chopped
2 cups chopped cooked ham
2 tablespoons ketchup
1 tablespoon Worcestershire sauce
1 cup thinly sliced green onions
½ teaspoon pepper
¼ teaspoon hot sauce

Sort and wash peas. Combine peas, ham hock, consommé, bay leaves, and 4 cups water in a Dutch oven. Bring to a boil; cover, reduce heat, and simmer 1 hour, stirring occasionally.

Add remaining 2 cups water, celery, and next 5 ingredients to pea mixture. Cover, reduce heat, and simmer 1 hour and 15 minutes or until peas and vegetables are tender.

Remove ham hock from stew; cool slightly. Remove meat from bone; discard fat and bone. Chop meat, and return to stew. Remove bay leaves.

Stir in green onions, pepper, and hot sauce; cook until thoroughly heated. **Yield: about 3 quarts.**

Minestrone

3 large potatoes, peeled and cut into cubes
2 small onions, chopped
6 carrots, scraped and cut into chunks
1 small zucchini, cut into chunks
2 cloves garlic, minced
1 (10-ounce) package frozen chopped spinach
2 cups rotini (corkscrew pasta)
1½ quarts water
1 (18-ounce) can tomato paste
1 cup water
1 (15-ounce) can red kidney beans, undrained
1 (8-ounce) can cut green beans, undrained
1 (8½-ounce) can English peas, undrained
1½ to 2 teaspoons dried oregano
1 teaspoon dried basil
½ teaspoon dried tarragon
½ teaspoon dried thyme
1 bay leaf
Grated Parmesan cheese

Combine first 8 ingredients in a large Dutch oven; bring to a boil. Cover, reduce heat, and simmer 10 minutes or until potatoes are tender.

Stir tomato paste and 1 cup water into potato mixture. Add kidney beans and next 7 ingredients; simmer 5 minutes.

Remove bay leaf. Sprinkle each serving with Parmesan cheese. **Yield: 5 quarts.**

Bama Brunswick Stew

1 (2½- to 3-pound) broiler-fryer
1 (2- to 2½-pound) boneless pork loin roast
1 (2-pound) beef chuck roast
2½ quarts water
3 large potatoes, peeled and finely chopped
3 large onions, finely chopped
1 (28-ounce) can tomatoes, undrained and
    chopped
1 (17-ounce) can cream-style corn
1 (14-ounce) bottle ketchup
1 small hot pepper
¼ cup dry red wine
2 to 3 tablespoons lemon juice
2 tablespoons dry sherry
1½ teaspoons paprika
1 teaspoon brown sugar
1 teaspoon black pepper
½ teaspoon ground red pepper
½ teaspoon dried red pepper flakes

Combine first 4 ingredients in a large Dutch oven; cover and bring to a boil. Reduce heat, and simmer 1 hour or until meat is tender.

Remove meat from broth, reserving broth. Cool meat completely. Remove meat from bones. Grind meat in food processor or food grinder. Skim fat from broth.

Add potato and onion to broth; cook over medium heat 20 to 25 minutes or until tender.

Add meat, tomato, and remaining ingredients; bring mixture to a boil. Reduce heat; simmer, uncovered, 2½ hours, stirring often. Add additional water for a thinner consistency, if desired. **Yield: 1½ gallons.**

Georgia Brunswick Stew

½ cup butter or margarine
3 cups chopped cooked chicken
3 cups chopped potato
2 cups chopped smoked pork (½ pound)
1 cup chopped onion
2 (14½-ounce) cans ready-to-serve chicken
    broth
2 (14½-ounce) cans stewed tomatoes
1 (16-ounce) can lima beans, drained
1 (17-ounce) can cream-style corn
1 (8½-ounce) can English peas, drained
¼ cup liquid smoke
Barbecue Sauce

Melt butter in a large Dutch oven. Stir in chicken and next 4 ingredients; bring to a boil. Reduce heat, and simmer, uncovered, 20 minutes.

Add tomatoes and remaining ingredients to Dutch oven; bring mixture to a boil. Reduce heat, and simmer, uncovered, 2 hours, stirring occasionally. **Yield: 3 quarts.**

Barbecue Sauce

¼ cup butter or margarine, melted
1¾ cups ketchup
¼ cup firmly packed brown sugar
¼ cup prepared mustard
¼ cup white vinegar
2 tablespoons Worcestershire sauce
1 to 2 tablespoons hot sauce
1 tablespoon liquid smoke
1½ teaspoons lemon juice
1½ teaspoons minced garlic
1 teaspoon coarsely ground black pepper
½ teaspoon crushed red pepper

Combine all ingredients in a large heavy saucepan. Cook over low heat 25 to 30 minutes, stirring often. **Yield: 1½ cups.**

Georgia Brunswick Stew

Virginia Brunswick Stew

Virginia Brunswick Stew

1 (3-pound) broiler-fryer
2 stalks celery, cut into 1-inch pieces
1 small onion, quartered
7 cups water, divided
2 (10-ounce) packages frozen baby lima beans
2 (10-ounce) packages frozen whole kernel corn
1 cup chopped onion
2 (28-ounce) cans whole tomatoes, undrained and chopped
1 (8-ounce) can whole tomatoes, undrained and chopped
3 medium potatoes, peeled and diced
2 tablespoons butter or margarine
1 tablespoon salt
1 to 1½ teaspoons black pepper
½ to 1 teaspoon ground red pepper
10 saltine crackers, crumbled

Combine broiler-fryer, celery, onion, and 5 cups water in a large Dutch oven or stockpot; bring to a boil. Cover, reduce heat, and simmer mixture 1 hour.

Remove chicken, celery, and onion from broth, reserving broth in Dutch oven; discard celery and onion. Cool chicken; skin, bone, and coarsely chop meat. Skim fat from broth.

Add chicken, lima beans, and next 9 ingredients to broth; bring to a boil. Reduce heat, and simmer, uncovered, about 4½ hours or until desired consistency, stirring often.

Add remaining 2 cups water as needed. Add cracker crumbs, and cook 15 additional minutes. **Yield: 3½ quarts.**

Brunswick Chicken Stew

1 (2½- to 3-pound) broiler-fryer
1 tablespoon salt
2 quarts water
¼ pound cooked pork or ham, cut into cubes
2 large onions, chopped
1 green pepper, seeded and chopped
2 tablespoons chopped fresh parsley
1 (16-ounce) can tomatoes, undrained and chopped
1 (16-ounce) can whole kernel corn, drained
1 (10-ounce) package frozen lima beans
1 (10-ounce) package frozen sliced okra
1 teaspoon salt
½ teaspoon black pepper
½ teaspoon dried thyme
1 bay leaf
1¼ teaspoons hot sauce

Combine first 3 ingredients in a large Dutch oven; bring to a boil. Cover, reduce heat, and simmer 1 hour.

Remove chicken from broth, reserving broth. Cool chicken; skin, bone, and coarsely chop meat. Skim fat from broth.

Combine 2 quarts reserved broth, chicken, pork, and remaining ingredients in a large Dutch oven. Cover and simmer 2 hours or until desired consistency, stirring often. Add broth or water for a thinner consistency, if desired. Remove bay leaf. **Yield: 1 gallon.**

Old-Fashioned Burgoo

Old-Fashioned Burgoo

1 cup dried Great Northern beans
¾ cup dried baby lima beans
¼ cup dried split peas
8 slices bacon, cut into 1-inch pieces
1 pound meaty beef or ham bones or 1 pound
      beef short ribs
1 (3-pound) broiler-fryer
1½ quarts water
2 large potatoes, peeled and chopped
1 large onion, chopped
1 large cooking apple, peeled and chopped
5 stalks celery with leaves, sliced
3 large carrots, scraped and sliced
2 large turnips, peeled and chopped
1 large green pepper, seeded and chopped
1 medium-size hot pepper, seeded
½ cup sliced okra
1 cup shredded cabbage
½ cup chopped fresh parsley
1 (8½-ounce) can English peas, undrained
1 (17-ounce) can whole kernel corn
3 (16-ounce) cans whole tomatoes, chopped
2 teaspoons salt
1 teaspoon pepper
¼ teaspoon ground red pepper
¼ teaspoon chili powder

Sort and wash beans and peas; place in a medium bowl. Cover with water 2 inches above beans; soak 8 hours.

Cook bacon in a large Dutch oven until crisp; remove bacon, and set aside. Drain pan drippings. Add soup bones, chicken, and water to Dutch oven. Bring to a boil; cover, reduce heat, and simmer 2 hours.

Remove chicken and soup bones from broth, reserving broth; cool meat completely. Bone and coarsely chop meat; set aside. Skim fat from broth.

Drain beans, and add to broth. Cover and cook over medium heat 30 minutes or until beans are almost tender.

Add chicken, bacon, potato, and remaining ingredients. Cover, reduce heat, and simmer 2 to 3 hours, stirring often. Add water for a thinner consistency, if desired. **Yield: about 1½ gallons.**

Burgoo for a Crowd

1 (2- to 2½-pound) pork loin roast
1 (2- to 2½-pound) broiler-fryer
3 quarts water
4 pounds ground beef
6 cups frozen whole kernel corn
5 cups frozen purple hull peas
5 cups frozen lima beans
3 cups chopped cabbage
2 medium potatoes, peeled and cubed
2 medium onions, chopped
1 (46-ounce) can tomato juice
1 (16-ounce) can whole tomatoes, undrained
      and chopped
2 cups frozen cut okra
1 pound carrots, scraped and diced
1 green pepper, seeded and chopped
¾ cup chopped celery
¼ cup chopped fresh parsley
1 to 2 tablespoons crushed red pepper
1 tablespoon salt
1 tablespoon celery salt
1½ teaspoons pepper

Combine first 3 ingredients in a large Dutch oven; bring to a boil. Cover, reduce heat, and simmer 2 hours.

Drain meat, reserving broth. Remove bone, and shred pork. Skin, bone, and shred chicken. Skim fat from broth. Return meat to broth.

Brown ground beef in a large skillet, stirring until it crumbles; drain. Add ground beef, corn, and remaining ingredients to broth; bring to a boil. Reduce heat, and simmer, uncovered, 2 hours; stir often. Add additional water for a thinner consistency, if desired. **Yield: 2½ gallons.**

Kentucky Burgoo

Kentucky Burgoo

1 (3- to 3½-pound) broiler-fryer
1 pound boneless beef
1 pound boneless veal
1 pound boneless pork
1 gallon water
3 medium potatoes, peeled and cubed
3 medium carrots, scraped and sliced
1 large onion, chopped
1 large green pepper, seeded and chopped
1 cup frozen cut okra
1 cup shredded cabbage
1 cup frozen whole kernel corn
1 cup frozen lima beans
1 cup chopped fresh parsley
½ cup finely chopped celery
1 hot red pepper
2 cups tomato puree
2 tablespoons salt
1 teaspoon red pepper
1 to 1½ teaspoons hot sauce

Combine broiler-fryer, beef, veal, pork, and water in a large Dutch oven; bring to a boil. Cover, reduce heat, and simmer 2 hours or until chicken and meat are tender.

Remove chicken and meat from broth, reserving broth; cool completely. Skin, bone, and chop chicken; discard skin. Coarsely chop meat, and set aside.

Skim fat from surface of broth. Measure broth, and return 3 quarts to Dutch oven.

Add chicken, meats, potato, and remaining ingredients; bring to a boil. Reduce heat, and simmer, uncovered, 4 hours, stirring often.

Add additional reserved broth and water, if necessary, to make desired consistency. Discard red pepper pod. **Yield: 5 quarts.**

Chilies, Gumbos & Jambalayas

Warm up the menu and stir up some fun with chilies, gumbos, and jambalayas. This collection of classic cold-weather specialties runs the gamut in ingredients and flavors.

Friday Night Chili, Five-Ingredient Chili, Hearty Kielbasa Chili

Spicy Seafood Gumbo, Savannah Snapper Gumbo, Creole Shrimp Jambalaya

Black Bean Chili Marsala, Bodacious Chili, Spicy Lamb and Black Bean Chili

Chicken-White Bean Chili, Vegetarian Chili, Microwave Gumbo

Cook-Off Chili (page 121)

Friday Night Chili

Friday Night Chili

2 pounds ground chuck
2 large onions, chopped
3 large cloves garlic, minced
2 (16-ounce) cans kidney beans, undrained
1 (16-ounce) can whole tomatoes, undrained and chopped
1 (8-ounce) can tomato sauce
2 cups water
1½ to 2 tablespoons chili powder
2 teaspoons garlic salt
1½ teaspoons ground cumin
1 teaspoon dried oregano
1 teaspoon black pepper
½ teaspoon ground red pepper
¼ teaspoon hot sauce
Condiments: corn chips, shredded sharp Cheddar cheese, sliced green onions

Cook first 3 ingredients in a Dutch oven over medium-high heat until meat is browned and onion is tender, stirring until meat crumbles. Drain well.

Stir in beans and next 10 ingredients. Bring to a boil; reduce heat, and simmer, uncovered, 1 hour, stirring occasionally. Serve chili with desired condiments. **Yield: 2¼ quarts.**

Chili Heritage

Chili owes much of its popularity to the introduction of chili powder in the 1890s by a Texan named William Gebhardt.

Five-Ingredient Chili

2 **pounds ground chuck**
1 **medium onion, chopped**
4 **(16-ounce) cans chili-hot beans, undrained**
2 **(1¾-ounce) packages chili seasoning mix**
1 **(46-ounce) can tomato juice**

Cook ground chuck and onion in a Dutch oven, stirring until meat crumbles; drain. Stir in beans and remaining ingredients.

Bring mixture to a boil; reduce heat, and simmer, uncovered, stirring occasionally, 2 hours. **Yield: 3½ quarts.**

Cook-Off Chili

(pictured on page 119)

2 **pounds ground beef**
½ **teaspoon chili powder**
¼ **teaspoon ground cumin**
2 **large onions, chopped**
4 **cloves garlic, minced**
1 **jalapeño pepper, seeded and chopped**
2 **tablespoons vegetable oil**
2 **(15-ounce) cans tomato sauce**
1 **(15½-ounce) can Mexican-style chili beans, undrained**
1½ **cups water**
1 **(6-ounce) can tomato paste**
½ **cup green chile salsa or jalapeño salsa**
3 to 4 **tablespoons chili powder**
1 **(16-ounce) can red kidney beans, drained**
1 **(12-ounce) can beer**
1 **(2¼-ounce) can sliced ripe olives, drained**
½ **teaspoon ground cumin**
Salt and pepper to taste
Hot sauce to taste
Condiments: shredded Cheddar cheese, sour cream, sliced ripe olives, tortilla chips

Cook first 3 ingredients in a Dutch oven, stirring until meat crumbles and browns. Drain and set aside.

Cook chopped onion, garlic, and jalapeño pepper in oil until tender. Stir in ground beef mixture, tomato sauce, and next 5 ingredients. Cover and simmer 20 minutes.

Add kidney beans and next 5 ingredients, stirring well; simmer 15 minutes. Serve chili with desired condiments. **Yield: 3½ quarts.**

Cook-Off Chili Techniques

Gloves are recommended when handling hot peppers. Capsaicin, the oil in the seeds and veins, is dangerously hot.

Simmer kidney beans gently over low heat since a rolling boil may cause them to lose their shape and texture.

Now, Thatsa Chili

2 pounds lean ground beef
1 pound hot Italian link sausage, casings removed
1 large onion, chopped
½ cup sliced fresh mushrooms
1½ tablespoons minced fresh garlic
¼ cup chili powder
2 to 3 tablespoons ground cumin
2 (16-ounce) cans Italian-style tomatoes, undrained and chopped
1 (16-ounce) can kidney beans, drained
1 (6-ounce) can tomato paste
⅔ cup beer
¼ cup chopped fresh parsley
¼ cup dry red wine
¼ cup Dijon mustard
1 tablespoon dried oregano
1 tablespoon dried basil
1 teaspoon salt
1 teaspoon pepper
2 tablespoons lemon juice
Condiments: shredded cheese, chopped green onions, commercial salsa, sour cream

Cook ground beef and sausage in a large Dutch oven, stirring until meat crumbles and browns. Drain; return to Dutch oven.

Add onion, mushrooms, and garlic; cook about 3 minutes, stirring constantly. Stir in chili powder and next 13 ingredients.

Bring to a boil; reduce heat, and simmer 1 to 2 hours, stirring occasionally. Serve with desired condiments. **Yield: 2¾ quarts.**

Hearty Kielbasa Chili

1 pound ground beef
½ pound kielbasa, cut into ½-inch slices
2 medium onions, chopped
2 cloves garlic, minced
1 (29-ounce) can tomato sauce
2 (15-ounce) cans red kidney beans, undrained
½ cup water
2 teaspoons chili powder
¼ teaspoon seasoned pepper
¼ teaspoon freshly ground black pepper

Cook first 4 ingredients in a Dutch oven, stirring until meat crumbles and browns; drain.

Stir in tomato sauce and remaining ingredients. Bring mixture to a boil; cover, reduce heat, and simmer chili 1 hour, stirring occasionally.
Yield: 2 quarts.

Black Bean Chili Marsala

1 large onion, chopped
2 cloves garlic, minced
3 tablespoons vegetable oil
1 (2½-pound) boneless beef chuck roast, trimmed and chopped
1 (29-ounce) can tomato sauce
2 (6-ounce) cans tomato paste
1 cup Marsala wine
1 cup water
2 or 3 (4-ounce) cans sliced mushrooms, drained
3 to 4 tablespoons chili powder
2 teaspoons seasoned salt
1 teaspoon freshly ground pepper
2 (15-ounce) cans black beans, undrained
Hot cooked rice
Garnish: strips of lime rind or cilantro sprigs

Cook onion and garlic in vegetable oil in a Dutch oven over medium-high heat, stirring constantly, until tender.

Add chopped roast and next 8 ingredients. Bring to a boil. Cover, reduce heat, and simmer 1 hour, stirring occasionally.

Add beans, and cook until thoroughly heated. Serve chili over hot cooked rice. Garnish, if desired. **Yield: 3 quarts.**

Note: You may substitute 1 cup dry white wine plus 1½ tablespoons brandy for Marsala wine.

Black Bean Chili Marsala

Chili con Carne

16 large dried red chiles
2½ quarts water
2 pounds round steak, cut into ½-inch cubes
3 tablespoons vegetable oil
1 large onion, chopped
2 cups water
2 cloves garlic, crushed
2 tablespoons chili powder
1 tablespoon ground cumin
1 teaspoon dried oregano
½ teaspoon salt
2 (16-ounce) cans ranch-style beans, undrained

Wash chiles, and place in a large Dutch oven; add 2½ quarts water. Cover and bring to a boil. Remove from heat, and let stand, covered, 45 minutes or until softened.

Drain chiles, reserving ½ cup soaking liquid. Wearing rubber gloves, pull off stems, slit chiles open, and rinse away seeds under running water.

Place half of chiles and ¼ cup soaking liquid in blender or food processor; cover and process until smooth. Repeat with remaining chiles and remaining ¼ cup soaking liquid. Press pureed mixture through a wire-mesh strainer, using the back of a spoon; set puree aside.

Brown steak in oil in Dutch oven. Add pureed mixture, onion, and next 6 ingredients. Cover and simmer 1½ hours. Add beans, and cook until heated thoroughly. **Yield: 1¾ quarts.**

From top: Chili Verde and Bodacious Chili

Chili Verde

¾ pound beef chuck roast, cut into 1-inch cubes
¾ pound pork loin or shoulder roast, cubed
1 large onion, chopped
1 large green pepper, seeded and chopped
1 clove garlic, minced
2 tablespoons olive oil, divided
2 (16-ounce) cans whole tomatoes, undrained
   and chopped
2 (4.5-ounce) cans chopped green chiles
1 cup dry red wine
1 cup commercial salsa
¼ cup chopped fresh cilantro
2 beef bouillon cubes
1 tablespoon brown sugar
3 tablespoons lemon juice
Hot cooked rice
Garnish: fresh cilantro sprigs

Combine first 5 ingredients. Cook half of mixture in 1 tablespoon olive oil in a large Dutch oven over medium-high heat, stirring constantly, until meat browns. Remove from Dutch oven; set aside. Repeat procedure with remaining meat mixture and 1 tablespoon olive oil.

Combine meat mixture, tomato, and next 7 ingredients. Bring to a boil; cover, reduce heat, and simmer 1 hour or until meat is tender, stirring occasionally. Serve over rice, and garnish, if desired. **Yield: 2¾ quarts.**

Bodacious Chili

2 pounds boneless beef chuck roast, cut into
    1-inch cubes
2 large onions, chopped
3 stalks celery, cut into 1-inch pieces
1 large green pepper, seeded and coarsely
    chopped
1 large sweet red pepper, seeded and coarsely
    chopped
1 cup sliced fresh mushrooms
2 jalapeño peppers, seeded and chopped
4 cloves garlic, minced
3 tablespoons olive oil
2 tablespoons cocoa
2 tablespoons chili powder
1 teaspoon ground cumin
1 teaspoon dried oregano
1 teaspoon paprika
1 teaspoon ground turmeric
½ teaspoon salt
½ teaspoon ground cardamom
¼ teaspoon pepper
1 tablespoon molasses
½ cup dry red wine
2 (16-ounce) cans whole tomatoes, undrained
    and chopped
1 (16-ounce) can kidney beans, drained
1 (16-ounce) can chick peas (garbanzo beans),
    drained
Spicy Sour Cream Topping
Shredded Cheddar cheese

Cook first 8 ingredients in olive oil in a large
Dutch oven over medium-high heat, stirring constantly, until meat browns. Drain and return meat
mixture to Dutch oven.

Stir in cocoa and next 13 ingredients. Bring
mixture to a boil; cover, reduce heat, and simmer
1½ hours, stirring occasionally.

Serve chili with Spicy Sour Cream Topping
and shredded Cheddar cheese. **Yield: 3 quarts.**

Spicy Sour Cream Topping

1 (8-ounce) carton sour cream
⅓ cup commercial salsa
2 tablespoons mayonnaise
1 teaspoon chili powder
½ teaspoon onion powder
½ teaspoon curry powder
Dash of ground red pepper
1 tablespoon lemon juice
1 teaspoon Dijon mustard

Combine all ingredients; cover and chill.
Serve with chili. **Yield: 1⅔ cups.**

Venison Chili

½ pound salt pork, quartered
2 pounds ground venison
2 medium onions, chopped
1 clove garlic, minced
1 (16-ounce) can whole tomatoes, undrained
    and coarsely chopped
1 cup water
¾ cup dry red wine
2 or 3 large green chiles, diced
3 tablespoons chili powder
¾ teaspoon dried oregano
½ teaspoon cumin seeds, crushed

Brown salt pork in a Dutch oven over medium
heat. Add venison, onion, and garlic; cook, stirring frequently, until venison crumbles and
browns. Drain.

Stir in tomato and remaining ingredients.
Bring to a boil; reduce heat, and simmer, uncovered, 1 hour, stirring occasionally. Remove salt
pork before serving. **Yield: 1½ quarts.**

Chicken-White Bean Chili

Sort and wash beans; place in a large Dutch oven. Cover with water 2 inches above beans. Soak 8 hours. Drain beans, and return to Dutch oven.

Add chicken broth and next 6 ingredients. Bring to a boil. Cover, reduce heat, and simmer 2 hours or until beans are tender, stirring occasionally.

Add chicken, green chiles, and 1 cup water. Cover and simmer 1 hour, stirring occasionally.

Make 4 cuts in each tortilla toward, but not through, center with kitchen shears. If desired, line serving bowls with tortillas, overlapping cut edges. Serve chili with desired condiments.
Yield: 3 quarts.

Chicken-White Bean Chili

1 pound dried navy beans
4 (14½-ounce) cans ready-to-serve chicken
    broth
1 large onion, chopped
2 cloves garlic, crushed
1 tablespoon pepper
1 tablespoon dried oregano
1 tablespoon ground cumin
1 teaspoon salt
5 cups chopped cooked chicken
1 (4.5-ounce) can chopped green chiles,
    drained
1 cup water
8 (8-inch) flour tortillas (optional)
Condiments: commercial salsa, sour cream,
    sliced green onions

Spicy Lamb and Black Bean Chili

1 pound ground lamb or turkey
½ cup chopped onion
Vegetable cooking spray
3 (8-ounce) cans no-salt-added tomato sauce
2 (15-ounce) cans black beans, drained
1 (14.5-ounce) can no-salt-added whole
    tomatoes, undrained and chopped
1 (16-ounce) can ready-to-serve chicken broth
2 (4.5-ounce) cans chopped green chiles,
    undrained
1½ tablespoons chili powder
2 teaspoons ground cumin
¼ teaspoon salt
¼ to ½ teaspoon ground red pepper

Cook meat and onion in a large Dutch oven coated with cooking spray over medium-high heat, stirring until meat crumbles and browns.

Add tomato sauce and remaining ingredients. Bring to a boil; reduce heat, and simmer 15 minutes, stirring occasionally. Yield: 2 quarts.

Turkey-Bean Chili

1 pound ground turkey
1 cup chopped onion
1 clove garlic, crushed
1 (15-ounce) can tomato sauce
1 (15½-ounce) can Mexican-style chili beans,
    undrained
¼ teaspoon salt
⅛ teaspoon pepper
2 tablespoons chili powder
1 tablespoon ground cumin
Condiments: commercial sour cream, chopped
    green onions, tortilla chips (optional)

Combine first 3 ingredients in a 3-quart baking dish. Cover and microwave at HIGH 5 to 6 minutes or until meat is no longer pink, stirring once; drain.

Add tomato sauce and next 5 ingredients. Cover and microwave at HIGH 10 to 12 minutes, stirring after 6 minutes. Serve with condiments, if desired. **Yield: 1¼ quarts.**

Turkey-Bean Chili

Turkey-Bean Chili Technique

To absorb fat and eliminate draining ground meat when microwaving, layer four white paper towels in a bowl. Microwave meat at HIGH; discard paper towels.

Vegetarian Chili

1 cup dried pinto beans
4 cups water
1 (17-ounce) can whole kernel corn,
    undrained
1 (15-ounce) can tomato sauce
1 large onion, chopped
1 (4.5-ounce) can chopped green chiles,
    drained
1 clove garlic, minced
1 teaspoon salt
2 teaspoons chili powder
1 teaspoon dried oregano
1 bay leaf
1 cup (4 ounces) shredded Monterey Jack
    cheese (optional)

Sort and wash beans; place in a Dutch oven. Cover with water 2 inches above beans; soak 8 hours. Drain beans, and return to Dutch oven.

Add 4 cups water and next 9 ingredients to Dutch oven. Bring to a boil; cover, reduce heat, and simmer 2½ hours or until beans are tender. Remove bay leaf. Serve with cheese, if desired. **Yield: about 2 quarts.**

Spicy Seafood Gumbo

1 cup vegetable oil
1 cup all-purpose flour
4 medium onions, chopped
8 stalks celery, chopped
3 cloves garlic, minced
4 (14½-ounce) cans ready-to-serve chicken
    broth
2 (28-ounce) cans whole tomatoes, undrained
    and chopped
2 (10-ounce) packages frozen sliced okra,
    thawed
1 pound crab claws
¼ cup Worcestershire sauce
1 tablespoon hot sauce
5 bay leaves
½ cup minced fresh parsley
2 teaspoons dried thyme
2 teaspoons dried basil
2 teaspoons dried oregano
2 teaspoons rubbed sage
1 teaspoon pepper
2 pounds unpeeled medium-size fresh shrimp
2 (12-ounce) containers Standard oysters,
    undrained
1 pound fresh crabmeat, drained and flaked
1 pound firm white fish fillets, cut into 1-inch
    cubes
Hot cooked rice
Gumbo filé (optional)

Combine oil and flour in a cast-iron skillet; cook over medium heat, stirring constantly, until roux is chocolate colored (about 20 minutes).

Stir in onion, celery, and garlic; cook 10 minutes, stirring frequently. Transfer mixture to a Dutch oven.

Add chicken broth and next 12 ingredients. Bring to a boil; reduce heat, and simmer, uncovered, 2 hours, stirring occasionally.

Peel shrimp, and devein, if desired. Add shrimp, oysters, crabmeat, and fish to Dutch oven. Bring to a boil; reduce heat, and simmer, uncovered, 10 minutes or until seafood is done. Remove bay leaves.

Serve gumbo over hot rice; sprinkle with gumbo filé, if desired. **Yield: 7 quarts.**

Spicy Seafood Gumbo Techniques

To make a roux, first whisk flour into oil.

Stir constantly until mixture becomes a light caramel color.

More cooking produces a rich, dark chocolate-colored roux.

Spicy Seafood Gumbo

Creole Gumbo

Creole Gumbo

1 cup vegetable oil
1 cup all-purpose flour
3 medium onions, chopped
3 green onions, chopped
2 large green peppers, seeded and chopped
2 stalks celery, sliced
4 cloves garlic, chopped
2 (16-ounce) cans Italian-style tomatoes, undrained and chopped
2 (10-ounce) packages frozen sliced okra, thawed
1 pound fully cooked Polish sausage, sliced
1 (6-ounce) can tomato paste
2 quarts water
4 bay leaves
3 tablespoons lemon juice
2 teaspoons dried thyme
1 teaspoon salt
¾ teaspoon pepper
½ teaspoon Creole seasoning
½ teaspoon ground red pepper
2 pounds unpeeled medium-size fresh shrimp
1 pound fresh crabmeat, drained and flaked
1 (12-ounce) container Standard oysters, undrained
⅓ cup chopped fresh parsley
Hot cooked rice

Combine oil and flour in a large Dutch oven; cook over medium heat, stirring constantly, until roux is chocolate colored (about 25 minutes).

Stir in onion, green onions, and next 3 ingredients; cook 3 to 5 minutes, stirring frequently.

Add tomato and next 11 ingredients. Bring to a boil; cover, reduce heat, and simmer 1½ hours, stirring occasionally. Remove bay leaves.

Peel shrimp, and devein, if desired. Stir in shrimp, crabmeat, oysters, and parsley; simmer 5 to 10 minutes or until shrimp turn pink and edges of oysters begin to curl.

Serve over hot cooked rice. **Yield: 6½ quarts.**

Microwave Gumbo

(pictured on page 2)

⅔ cup vegetable oil
⅔ cup all-purpose flour
2 cups sliced okra
1 cup chopped onion
1 cup chopped celery
½ cup chopped green pepper
2 cloves garlic, minced
2 (10½-ounce) cans condensed chicken broth
1½ cups water
1 (16-ounce) can whole tomatoes, drained and chopped
2 tablespoons Worcestershire sauce
1 to 2 teaspoons hot sauce
½ teaspoon paprika
½ teaspoon dried thyme
¼ teaspoon ground mace
1 pound unpeeled medium-size fresh shrimp
2 cups chopped cooked chicken or turkey
1 (12-ounce) container Standard oysters, drained
Hot cooked rice

Combine oil and flour in a deep 3-quart baking dish; stir well. Microwave, uncovered, at HIGH 6 minutes, stirring after 3 minutes. Stir well. Microwave, uncovered, at HIGH 2 to 4 minutes or until caramel colored, stirring every 30 seconds.

Stir in okra and next 4 ingredients. Cover with heavy-duty plastic wrap; fold back a small edge of wrap to allow steam to escape. Microwave at HIGH 4 to 5 minutes or until tender.

Stir in chicken broth and next 7 ingredients. Cover and microwave at HIGH 13 to 15 minutes or until boiling, stirring after 8 minutes.

Peel shrimp. Add shrimp, chicken, and oysters. Reduce to MEDIUM HIGH (70% power); cover and microwave 8 to 10 minutes or until shrimp turn pink and edges of oysters begin to curl.

Serve gumbo over hot cooked rice. **Yield: about 3 quarts.**

Southern Seafood Gumbo

½ cup vegetable oil
½ cup all-purpose flour
4 stalks celery, chopped
2 medium onions, chopped
1 small green pepper, seeded and chopped
1 clove garlic, minced
½ pound okra, sliced
1 tablespoon vegetable oil
1 quart ready-to-serve chicken broth
1 quart water
¼ cup Worcestershire sauce
1 teaspoon hot sauce
¼ cup ketchup
1 small tomato, chopped
1 teaspoon salt
2 slices bacon or 1 small ham slice, chopped
1 bay leaf
¼ teaspoon dried thyme
¼ teaspoon dried rosemary
¼ teaspoon red pepper flakes
2 pounds unpeeled medium-size fresh shrimp
2 cups chopped cooked chicken
1 pound fresh crabmeat, drained and flaked
1 (12-ounce) container Standard oysters,
    undrained (optional)
Hot cooked rice
Gumbo filé (optional)

Combine ½ cup oil and flour in a large Dutch oven; cook over medium heat, stirring constantly, until roux is caramel colored (15 to 20 minutes). Stir in celery and next 3 ingredients; cook 45 minutes, stirring occasionally.

Fry okra in 1 tablespoon hot oil until browned. Add to gumbo, and stir well over low heat for a few minutes. (At this stage, the mixture may be cooled, packaged, and frozen or refrigerated for later use.)

Add chicken broth and next 11 ingredients. Bring to a boil; reduce heat, and simmer, uncovered, 2½ hours, stirring occasionally.

Peel shrimp, and devein, if desired. Add shrimp, chicken, crabmeat, and oysters, if desired, during last 10 minutes of simmering period. Remove bay leaf.

Serve over rice. Sprinkle with gumbo filé, if desired. **Yield: 3½ quarts.**

Make a Roux

You can prepare a roux using the traditional procedure (pictured on page 128), or you can eliminate the fat from the roux by using the conventional oven method. A third and quicker method is to prepare the roux in your microwave.

To make an oven roux: Place ¾ cup all-purpose flour in a 13- x 9- x 2-inch pan. Bake at 400° for 15 to 20 minutes, stirring every 4 minutes. Flour will be the color of caramel. Yield: enough roux for 1 gallon gumbo.

To make a microwave roux: Combine ¾ cup vegetable oil and ¾ cup all-purpose flour in a 4-cup glass measure, stirring until mixture is blended. Microwave at HIGH 6 minutes; stir and microwave at HIGH 2 minutes. Stir mixture, and continue microwaving at HIGH 1 to 3 minutes, stirring at 1-minute intervals until mixture turns the color of caramel or chocolate. (Roux continues to brown as it cools; do not overcook.) Yield: enough roux for 1 gallon gumbo.

Catfish Gumbo

Catfish Gumbo

1 cup chopped green pepper
1 cup chopped celery
1 cup chopped onion
2 cloves garlic, minced
¼ cup vegetable oil
2 (14½-ounce) cans ready-to-serve beef broth
1 (16-ounce) can whole tomatoes, undrained
    and chopped
1 teaspoon salt
½ teaspoon dried oregano
½ teaspoon dried thyme
½ teaspoon red pepper
1 bay leaf
2 pounds farm-raised catfish fillets
1 (10-ounce) package frozen sliced okra,
    thawed
Hot cooked rice

Cook first 4 ingredients in oil in a Dutch oven, stirring constantly, until tender. Stir in beef broth and next 6 ingredients. Bring to a boil; cover, reduce heat, and simmer 30 minutes, stirring occasionally.

Cut catfish into 1-inch pieces; add to gumbo, and simmer 10 minutes. Stir in okra; cook 5 minutes. Remove bay leaf.

Serve gumbo over hot cooked rice. **Yield: about 3½ quarts.**

Savannah Snapper Gumbo

3 tablespoons vegetable oil
2 tablespoons all-purpose flour
1 medium-size green pepper, seeded and
    chopped
1 stalk celery, chopped
1 medium onion, chopped
1 (14½-ounce) can stewed tomatoes
1 (14½-ounce) can ready-to-serve chicken
    broth
1 (10-ounce) package frozen sliced okra
1 (10-ounce) package frozen whole kernel
    corn
1 cup water
1 tablespoon Worcestershire sauce
½ teaspoon salt
¼ teaspoon ground red pepper
⅛ teaspoon dried thyme
1 bay leaf
12 ounces fresh red snapper fillets, cubed
Hot cooked rice

Combine oil and flour with a wire whisk in a Dutch oven; cook over medium heat, stirring constantly, until caramel colored (10 to 15 minutes).

Stir in green pepper, celery, and onion. Cook over medium heat, stirring occasionally, about 10 minutes or until vegetables are tender.

Add tomatoes and next 9 ingredients. Bring to a boil; reduce heat, and simmer 10 minutes.

Stir in red snapper, and cook 5 minutes. Remove bay leaf.

Serve over hot cooked rice. **Yield: 2 quarts.**

Chicken and Sausage Gumbo

Chicken and Sausage Gumbo

1½ pounds smoked sausage or andouille
1 (3½- to 4-pound) broiler-fryer, cut up and
    skinned
¼ cup vegetable oil
½ cup all-purpose flour
2 large onions, minced
1 large green pepper, seeded and minced
1 cup minced celery
3 cloves garlic, minced
2 quarts water
2 teaspoons Creole seasoning
⅛ teaspoon hot sauce
½ cup chopped green onions
¼ cup minced fresh parsley
Hot cooked rice

Cut sausage lengthwise into 4 pieces; cut pieces into ½-inch slices. Brown in a Dutch oven. Drain; reserve drippings in pan. Set sausage aside. Brown chicken in drippings; drain and set aside.

Combine oil and flour in Dutch oven; cook over medium heat, stirring constantly, until roux is chocolate colored (25 to 30 minutes).

Add onion and next 3 ingredients; cook until vegetables are tender. Add water; bring to a boil. Reduce heat, and simmer, uncovered, 45 minutes.

Add chicken, Creole seasoning, and hot sauce; cook, uncovered, 1 hour.

Remove chicken, and set aside to cool. Add green onions and parsley to gumbo. Bone chicken, and coarsely chop. Add chicken and sausage to gumbo; heat thoroughly.

Ladle gumbo into bowls. Pack hot cooked rice into greased custard cups; invert into bowls of gumbo, or serve gumbo over hot cooked rice.
Yield: about 3 quarts.

Note: To remove fat from surface, cover and chill 8 hours. Remove fat; reheat gumbo, and serve. For a more traditional gumbo, leave chicken pieces intact.

Duck, Oyster, and Sausage Gumbo

2 large wild ducks, cleaned
2 stalks celery with leaves, cut into 2-inch
    pieces
1 medium onion, sliced
1 tablespoon salt
Chicken broth
1 pound hot smoked sausage, cut into 1-inch
    pieces
½ cup vegetable oil
½ cup all-purpose flour
¾ cup finely chopped celery
1 large onion, finely chopped
1 green pepper, seeded and finely chopped
Salt and pepper to taste
6 green onions with tops, finely chopped
2 tablespoons chopped fresh parsley
1 (12-ounce) container Standard oysters,
    undrained
Hot cooked rice
Gumbo filé

Combine first 4 ingredients in a large Dutch oven; cover with water. Bring to a boil; cover, reduce heat, and simmer about 1 hour or until ducks are tender.

Remove ducks from stock, reserving stock. Let ducks cool; remove meat from bones, and cut into bite-size pieces. Set aside.

Return skin and bones to stock; cover and simmer 1 hour. Pour stock through a wire-mesh strainer into a large bowl, discarding solids. Add enough chicken broth to make 2½ quarts liquid; set aside.

Cook sausage in a skillet over medium heat about 5 minutes, stirring occasionally. Drain on paper towels, and set aside.

Heat oil in a 5-quart heavy cast-iron pot or Dutch oven; stir in flour. Cook over medium heat, stirring constantly, until roux is chocolate colored (about 25 minutes).

Add chopped celery, chopped onion, and green pepper; cook over medium heat 10 minutes, stirring constantly.

Remove from heat, and gradually stir in reserved hot stock. Bring mixture to a boil; reduce heat, and simmer 20 minutes.

Add duck, sausage, salt, and pepper to stock mixture; simmer 20 minutes. Stir in green onions and parsley; simmer 20 minutes. Add oysters; simmer 10 minutes.

Serve gumbo over hot cooked rice. Sprinkle with gumbo filé. **Yield: 8 to 10 servings.**

Note: Gumbo is best when made a day ahead, chilled, and reheated.

Turkey and Sausage Gumbo

1 pound smoked sausage, cut into ½-inch
    slices
¼ cup vegetable oil
¼ cup all-purpose flour
3 stalks celery, chopped
2 medium onions, chopped
2 cups cubed cooked turkey
3 cups water
½ teaspoon salt
¼ teaspoon pepper
Hot cooked rice
Gumbo filé

Brown sausage in a large skillet over medium heat; drain and set aside.

Combine oil and flour in a Dutch oven; cook over medium heat, stirring constantly, until roux is caramel colored (about 10 minutes). Add celery and onion; cook until tender, stirring frequently.

Add sausage, turkey, and water. Bring to a boil; reduce heat, and simmer, uncovered, 2 hours, stirring occasionally. Stir in salt and pepper.

Serve gumbo over rice; sprinkle with gumbo filé, if desired. **Yield: 1½ quarts.**

Wild Game Gumbo

2 quarts water
1 (2½- to 3-pound) broiler-fryer
1½ teaspoons salt
8 dove breasts (about 1 pound)
1 pound venison roast, cut into 1-inch cubes
1 squirrel, dressed and cut into pieces (optional)
1 rabbit, dressed and quartered (about 2 pounds)
2 quail, dressed
1 small onion
1 stalk celery
1 bay leaf
1 tablespoon salt
¼ teaspoon red pepper
1½ pounds smoked link sausage, cut into ½-inch slices
¼ cup bacon drippings
½ cup all-purpose flour
1 cup chopped onion
1 cup chopped celery
2 to 3 teaspoons pepper
1 teaspoon hot sauce
½ teaspoon ground red pepper
1 teaspoon Worcestershire sauce
Hot cooked rice

Combine first 3 ingredients in a large Dutch oven. Bring to a boil; cover, reduce heat, and simmer 1 hour or until tender.

Remove chicken from broth. Chill broth; remove fat from broth. Skin, bone, and coarsely chop chicken. Set aside.

Combine dove breasts and next 8 ingredients (or 9, if you add squirrel) in large Dutch oven; add water to cover. Bring to a boil; cover, reduce heat, and simmer 2 hours.

Remove meat from broth; strain broth. Set aside. Remove meat from bones, and chop into bite-size pieces. Set aside.

Brown sausage in a large heavy skillet over medium heat. Drain on paper towels, leaving drippings in skillet.

Add bacon drippings to skillet. Heat over medium heat until hot. Add flour, and cook, stirring constantly, until roux is caramel colored (15 to 20 minutes.) Add chopped onion, celery, and pepper; cook 10 minutes.

Combine roux and reserved chicken broth in large Dutch oven; cover and simmer 30 minutes. Add game, sausage, chicken, hot sauce, red pepper, and Worcestershire sauce.

Add reserved stock from game if additional liquid is desired; simmer, uncovered, 2 hours, stirring occasionally. Serve over hot cooked rice.
Yield: 4½ quarts.

Dove and Sausage Gumbo

15 dove breasts
1 (10½-ounce) can beef consommé, undiluted
1 beef-flavored bouillon cube
½ cup vegetable oil
½ cup all-purpose flour
1½ cups finely chopped onion
1 cup finely chopped celery
2 cloves garlic, minced
1 or 2 bay leaves
2 tablespoons Worcestershire sauce
½ teaspoon dried basil
¼ teaspoon poultry seasoning
¼ teaspoon freshly ground black pepper
⅛ teaspoon ground red pepper
⅛ teaspoon ground allspice
⅛ teaspoon ground cloves
¾ pound smoked sausage, cut into ¼-inch slices
¼ cup dry red wine
⅛ teaspoon hot sauce
Hot cooked rice
Gumbo filé (optional)

Place dove breasts in a Dutch oven; add water to cover. Bring to a boil; cover, reduce heat, and simmer 10 minutes.

Remove dove from broth, reserving broth. Let dove cool. Bone and coarsely chop dove; set aside. Add enough water to reserved broth to measure 3 cups, if necessary.

Combine broth, consommé, and bouillon cube in a medium saucepan; cook over medium heat until bouillon cube dissolves. Set aside.

Brown dove in oil in Dutch oven over medium heat. Remove dove, reserving drippings in Dutch oven; add flour to drippings. Cook over medium heat, stirring constantly, until roux is caramel colored (about 15 minutes).

Add 1½ cups broth gradually; cook over medium heat, stirring constantly, until mixture is thickened and bubbly.

Add onion and celery to roux mixture; cook 5 minutes or until vegetables are tender, stirring occasionally. Add remaining broth, garlic, and next 8 ingredients; stir well.

Brown sausage in a large skillet over medium heat. Add sausage and dove to roux mixture. Bring to a boil; cover, reduce heat, and simmer 1½ hours, stirring occasionally.

Stir in wine and hot sauce. Remove bay leaves. Serve gumbo over rice; sprinkle with gumbo filé, if desired. **Yield: 1¼ quarts.**

Okra Gumbo

1 large onion, chopped
1 large green pepper, seeded and chopped
2 tablespoons vegetable oil or bacon drippings
4 cups sliced fresh okra
3 ripe tomatoes, peeled and chopped
1 cup corn cut from cob (about 2 ears)
1 tablespoon white vinegar
½ teaspoon salt
¼ teaspoon black pepper
⅛ teaspoon ground red pepper

Cook onion and green pepper in oil in a Dutch oven, stirring constantly, until tender. Add okra and remaining ingredients, and cook over medium heat 15 minutes, stirring frequently. Serve immediately. **Yield: 1½ quarts.**

Ground Beef Gumbo

1½ pounds ground beef
⅔ cup chopped onion
⅔ cup chopped celery
⅔ cup chopped green pepper
2 or 3 cloves garlic, minced
1 (16-ounce) can whole tomatoes, undrained and chopped
1 (15-ounce) can tomato sauce
2 (6-ounce) cans tomato paste
1 (6-ounce) jar sliced mushrooms, drained
2½ cups frozen sliced okra
2 bay leaves
1½ tablespoons dried parsley flakes
2½ teaspoons Italian seasoning
1½ teaspoons dried basil
1 teaspoon dried oregano
1 teaspoon chili powder
1 teaspoon onion powder
½ teaspoon cumin powder
Salt and pepper to taste
½ cup water
2 tablespoons dry red wine
Hot cooked rice

Cook first 5 ingredients in a heavy Dutch oven over medium heat, stirring until meat crumbles and browns; drain.

Stir in tomato and next 15 ingredients. Bring to a boil; reduce heat, and simmer, uncovered, 1 hour. Remove bay leaves. Serve over hot cooked rice. **Yield: 1¼ quarts.**

Creole Jambalaya

1½ pounds unpeeled medium-size fresh
　　shrimp
¾ cup chopped onion
½ cup chopped celery
¼ cup chopped green pepper
1 tablespoon minced fresh parsley
1 clove garlic, minced
2 tablespoons butter or margarine, melted
1 (28-ounce) can whole tomatoes, undrained
　　and chopped
1 (10½-ounce) can condensed beef broth,
　　undiluted
1¼ cups water
½ teaspoon dried thyme
½ teaspoon chili powder
¼ teaspoon pepper
2 cups cubed cooked ham
1 cup long-grain rice, uncooked

Peel shrimp, and devein, if desired. Set aside.

Cook onion and next 4 ingredients in butter in a Dutch oven over medium-high heat, stirring constantly, until vegetables are tender.

Stir in tomato and next 6 ingredients. Bring to a boil; stir in rice. Cover, reduce heat, and simmer 25 minutes.

Add shrimp to rice mixture. Bring to a boil; cover, reduce heat, and simmer 10 minutes or until shrimp turn pink. **Yield: 6 servings.**

Hearty Fare

Gumbos and jambalayas may contain one or more kinds of seafood, chicken or other poultry, or combinations of pork, seafood, and sausage. Gumbos are served over rice; jambalayas have rice as an ingredient.

Creole Shrimp Jambalaya

1½ pounds unpeeled medium-size fresh
　　shrimp
2 tablespoons vegetable oil
1 cup chopped onion
½ cup chopped green pepper
1 carrot, scraped and cut into thin strips
½ cup chopped celery
3 cloves garlic, minced
1 (8-ounce) can tomato sauce
1 (16-ounce) can whole tomatoes, undrained
　　and chopped
1 (14½-ounce) can ready-to-serve chicken
　　broth
1¼ cups water
1 cup long-grain rice, uncooked
1 teaspoon salt
½ teaspoon dried thyme
½ teaspoon red pepper
¼ teaspoon chili powder
¼ teaspoon sugar
½ cup chopped fresh parsley
⅛ teaspoon hot sauce (optional)

Peel shrimp, and devein, if desired. Cook shrimp in oil in a small Dutch oven over medium heat, stirring constantly, 5 minutes or until shrimp turn pink. Remove shrimp with a slotted spoon; cover and chill.

Add onion and next 4 ingredients to Dutch oven; cook over medium heat 3 minutes.

Stir in tomato sauce and next 9 ingredients. Bring to a boil; cover, reduce heat, and simmer, stirring frequently, 45 minutes or until rice is tender and most of liquid is absorbed.

Stir in parsley and shrimp; cook about 10 minutes or until thoroughly heated. Add hot sauce, if desired. **Yield: 4 servings.**

Creole Shrimp Jambalaya

Black-Eyed Pea Jambalaya

Black-Eyed Pea Jambalaya

1½ cups dried black-eyed peas
4 (10½-ounce) cans condensed chicken broth, undiluted
2 medium tomatoes, chopped
2 cloves garlic, minced
1 medium-size green pepper, seeded and chopped
1 small onion, chopped
1 stalk celery, chopped
1 bay leaf
1 cup cubed cooked ham
½ teaspoon salt
¼ teaspoon dried thyme
⅛ teaspoon ground cloves
1½ cups long-grain rice, uncooked
½ cup sliced green onions
1½ teaspoons hot sauce
Garnish: fresh thyme sprigs

Sort and wash peas; place in a 6-quart pressure cooker. Add water to chicken broth to make 5 cups.

Add broth, tomato, and next 9 ingredients to peas; stir well. Close lid securely. According to manufacturer's directions, bring to high pressure over high heat (about 10 to 12 minutes). Reduce heat to medium or level needed to maintain high pressure; cook 15 minutes.

Remove from heat; run cold water over cooker to reduce pressure rapidly. Remove lid so that steam escapes away from you.

Drain pea mixture, reserving 3 cups liquid. Remove bay leaf. Remove pea mixture from cooker; set aside, and keep warm.

Add rice and reserved liquid to cooker; stir gently. Close lid securely; bring to high pressure over high heat (about 5 minutes). Reduce heat to medium or level needed to maintain high pressure; cook 5 minutes.

Remove from heat; run cold water over cooker to reduce pressure rapidly. Remove lid so that steam escapes away from you.

Stir in pea mixture, green onions, and hot sauce. Garnish, if desired. **Yield: 6 servings.**

Good Luck Jambalaya

½ cup salt pork strips
2 cloves garlic, minced
1 large onion, chopped
1 medium-size green pepper, seeded and chopped
2 (16-ounce) cans black-eyed peas with jalapeño peppers, undrained
⅔ cup Bloody Mary mix
⅓ cup long-grain rice, uncooked
1 pound unpeeled medium-size fresh shrimp

Cook salt pork in a large skillet, stirring constantly, until golden. Add garlic, onion, and green pepper, and cook, stirring constantly, until tender.

Add peas, Bloody Mary mix, and rice. Bring to a boil over medium heat; cover, reduce heat, and simmer 20 minutes.

Peel shrimp, and devein, if desired. Add shrimp; cover jambalaya, and cook 5 minutes or until shrimp turn pink.

Serve immediately. **Yield: 6 to 8 servings.**

Index